ALIEN EMPIRE

AN EXPLORATION OF THE LIVES OF INSECTS

ALIEN EMPIRE

Christopher O'Toole

T 19916

HarperCollinsPublishers

Acknowledgements

I thank my partner, Rose Underwood, for her love and constant support during the writing of this book and for reading the entire manuscript with a non-specialist's eye. I am grateful to Steve Nicholls for many useful discussions which were helpful in developing the concept for this book. I thank the editorial team of Sheila Ableman, Martha Caute, Christine King and Jennifer Fry of BBC Books for their skilled and patient help.

First published by BBC Books,
an imprint of BBC Worldwide Publishing
BBC Worldwide Limited, Woodlands,
80 Wood Lane, London W12 0TT

FIRST EDITION

Library of Congress Cataloging-in-Publication Data available upon request.

ISBN 0-06-270156-8

95 96 97 98 99 CL 10 9 8 7 6 5 4 3 2 1

Photographs on the preceding pages:

PAGE 1: *A mustachioed nightmare, this lymantriid moth caterpillar (South Africa) signals its distasteful nature with its warningly coloured face.*

PAGE 2: *A nymph of the praying mantis,* Polyspilota aeruginosa *(Madagascar), rears up in a defensive display, showing the heavily spined raptorial legs used in prey capture.*

*This book is for
Rose, my love*

LEFT: *A green patch
swallowtail butterfly,* Papilio
phorcas, *roosts in a Kenyan
rainforest.*

CONTENTS

PREFACE

INSECTS ARE EVERYWHERE and we need them. While many people in the over-developed world see insects as objects of disgust, we all depend on them for the largely unseen ecological services performed by these much-maligned, but often strikingly beautiful, animals.

Insects deserve a better press: very few of them are actually real pests or disseminators of disease. We need to know more about them, to understand more of their intricate roles in maintaining our planet's life-support systems. And if we are to continue to benefit from insects, then we have to know how our own depredations on the world's eco-systems are likely to affect them. In short, we need to know more about insects so that we are better placed to conserve them and, ultimately, our own living space.

It is true that the world would be a sadder place without those beautiful and threatened star species of the conservation movement, the giant panda, the Siberian tiger and the blue whale. We must save them. But we need to expand our conservation ethics to embrace those unsung toilers on whom we depend, the insects.

I was delighted when Steve Nicholls, executive producer of the BBC series *Alien Empire*, asked me to be scientific consultant. And I was doubly pleased to be asked to write this, the book of the series: both gave me the chance to contribute to something near and dear to me, namely the popularization of insects.

If this sounds like unashamed bias, then I am happy to confess to it. I have been lucky enough to have made a career out of studying insects and helping to curate one of the world's greatest collections of them. After working with insects for nearly 30 years, they still excite and intrigue me.

Christopher O'Toole

Hope Entomological Collections,
University Museum, Oxford

OPPOSITE: *A bush cricket (katydid),* Amblycorypha floridiana *(Florida, USA), feeds on a leaf. Normally bright green, this individual is a rare, pink mutant.*

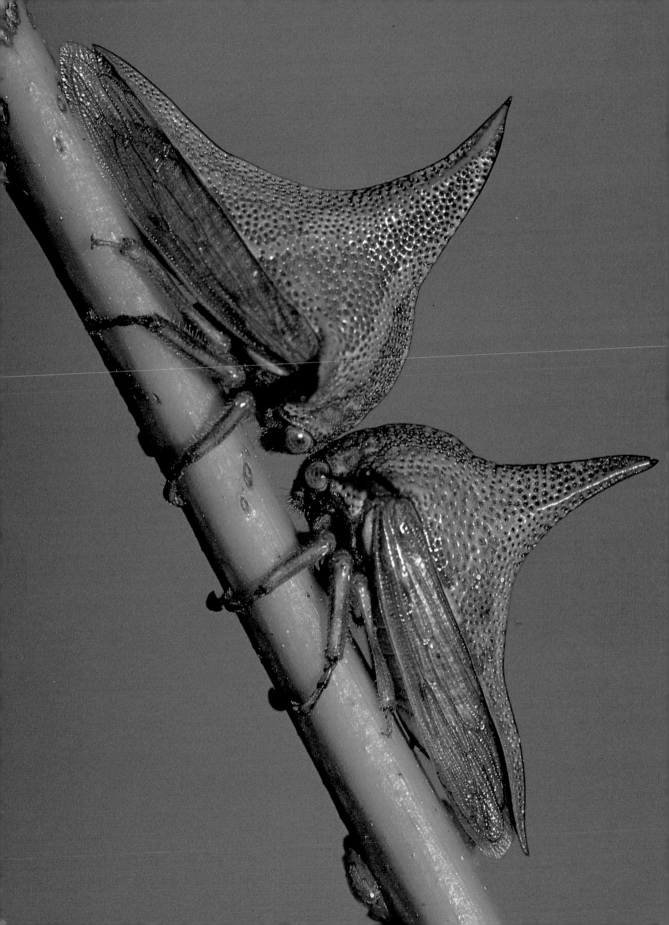

INTRODUCTION

W<small>E TALK OF THE</small> age of the Ruling Reptiles, when dinosaurs ruled the world. We like to think that we humans have inherited this pre-eminent position. But, in truth, both dinosaurs and humans were able to live and prosper by courtesy of the insects, the real rulers of the world. These armour-plated little creatures really do make the world go round. And they have been doing it for at least 300 million years.

If this sounds like exaggeration, let's take a reality check. Insects are everywhere, performing most of the major ecological tasks upon which we and all other land animals depend; they occupy key positions in all food chains. Insects process and dispose of organic matter, returning valuable nutrients to the soil. All our fruits and many of our vegetables depend entirely on the pollination services of insects, especially bees.

Insects may decimate crops and transmit disease, yet other insects, such as predatory beetles and parasitic wasps, do much to keep overall numbers in check. Even so, insects exist in vast numbers. There are over a million described species; some estimates place the number of species at between 15 and 30 million. Indeed, insects are so numerous that their swarming hordes are prey for a wide range of other animals too, from spiders and scorpions, lizards and birds, to many mammals, including people. Insects are so numerous and reliable a source of food that many animals specialize on them exclusively.

If we convert the insect phenomenon into a numbers game, then it soon becomes mind-numbing: the biomass (total weight) of ants and termites in the Amazon basin accounts for one-third of the total for all animals in the area, including people. A swarm of the African desert locust, *Schistocerca gregaria*, may comprise 50 000 million individuals, occupy up to 1000 square kilometres and take six hours to pass an observer on the ground. The worker bees of a single hive may make 2–3 million flower visits per day; the foraging area of such a colony may be 2–300 square kilometres. There are about 10 000 million insects per square kilometre of habitable land, or, to put it another way, there are 200 million individuals for every human being living today.

With insects dominating the ecological numbers game in this way, there is no denying their importance for life on this planet. Indeed, they are the most successful animals of all time. And this book is an exploration and celebration of that success.

OPPOSITE: *Two female thornbugs,* Umbonia crassicornis *(Florida, USA), face-to-face on a stem.*

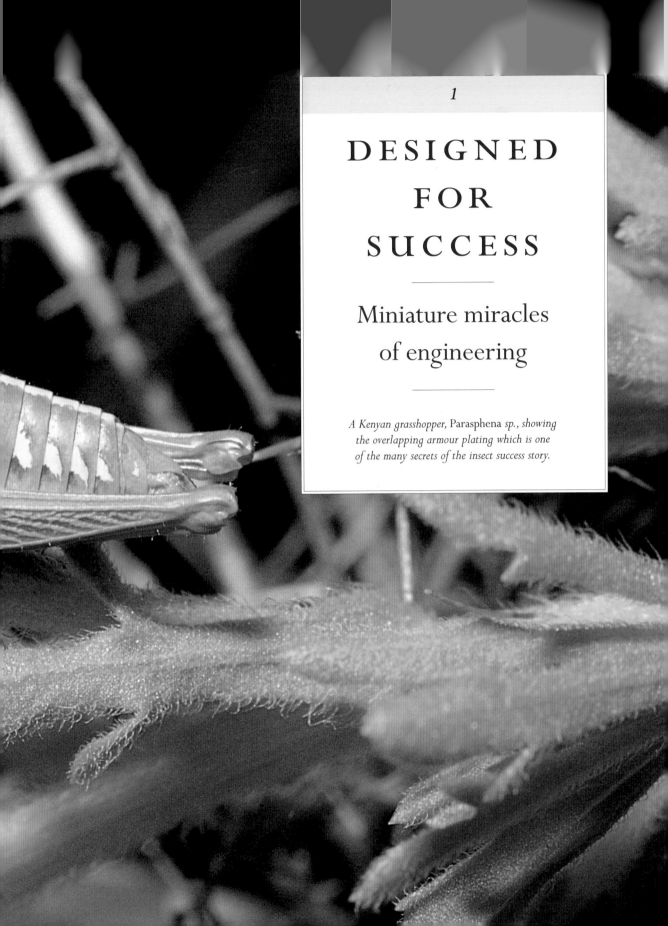

DESIGNED FOR SUCCESS

Miniature miracles
of engineering

A Kenyan grasshopper, Parasphena *sp., showing
the overlapping armour plating which is one
of the many secrets of the insect success story.*

I MAGINE YOU ARE the chief executive of a high-tech engineering firm, at the cutting edge of robot technology. Your chief designer presents you with an idea for a new project. How would you react if that project was nothing less than to design a million or more types of robot, with the following specifications?

Hardware:

* Armour-plated, miniature, self-replicating robots, with the ability to colonize almost all terrestrial habitats and dominate almost all available resources.

* Most kinds will be able to fly, and many will also be fast runners and/or jumpers.

* Many types will have two or more construction phases, each of which will operate in a different habitat from the finished product.

* All will have on-board sensors for gathering visual, auditory and scent data and transmitters for emitting sound, scent and, in some cases, light signals.

* Many examples will be capable of prosecuting chemical warfare, using either compounds gathered from plants or substances manufactured themselves.

* All robots will generate their own energy by using resources of animal and/or plant origin. Some will exploit resources in collaboration with a range of fungi, bacteria or single-celled animals.

* Some kinds of robot will be programmed to steal components from other robots and incorporate them into their own structures.

* Many types will be programmed to function in co-operating groups. These will construct and maintain their own micro-habitats, using building materials manufactured chemically themselves and/or materials gathered from the environment.

Software:

* All types will have an on-board computer with software capable of processing and integrating visual and chemical signals. Some will also be able to process audio signals.

* All software will be time-sensitive, with adequate memory storage space.

You may conclude that these specifications are the product of a diseased mind, the effusions of a mad scientist with delusions of grandeur and infinite resources. But you would be wrong. Such self-replicating robots, with precisely these specifications, do exist. They have dominated the earth for at least 300 million years. Their interactions with plants made our humanity possible. We call these robots insects. And without them, we would die.

BASIC BLUEPRINTS: ARMOUR PLATING

Like us, insects have a supporting framework, the skeleton. It supports tissues, and muscles move it. But there, the similarities end: unlike ours, an insect's skeleton is on the outside of the body, forming an enclosing shell or cuticle of linked, articulating, armour plates. The basic plan is therefore a cylinder. And because a cylinder has great structural strength, insects have no need of rigid spine or backbone. As it is on the outside, the insect skeleton is called an exoskeleton. (Ours is called an endoskeleton, for obvious reasons.)

Spines plus armour plating make this larva of a net-veined beetle, Dulticola *sp. (Borneo), a tough mouthful.*

The insect skeleton is not made of bone; it comprises a horny substance called chitin, combined with proteins. If this had been invented by a materials scientist, he would be a millionaire many times over: chitin is a truly amazing multi-purpose substance, which combines lightness with great strength. It has enabled insects to arrive at elegant solutions to engineering problems. Within the same insect, chitin can exist in different forms: it can be very solid, rigid and impermeable to liquids and gases, and form tough structures such as the sharp cutting edges of jaws; it can also be thin and flexible without losing strength, and this provides the hinging between areas of armour plating. And, if necessary, it *can* be permeable to liquids and gases, as in gills.

Chitin is extremely mouldable, enabling insects to evolve a remarkable range of external shapes without compromising the basic

functions: external protection and internal support for muscles and other tissues.

The multi-purpose nature of chitin-based cuticle is highlighted by the wide range of structures made of it. Apart from the exoskeleton, these include the linings of the fore- and hindguts and the tracheal breathing tubes; the protective spines of crickets and beetles, the furry coats of bees and some flies, and the minute scales which give butterfly and moth wings their colour patterns. All sense organs are made of highly modified cuticle, including the lenses of eyes and the perforated hairs involved in perceiving taste and smell.

The wonderful range of insect colours is also cuticle-based. Most colours are based on pigments laid down in the cuticle. The pigments may be manufactured by the insects themselves, or sequestered from food plants.

The brilliant, metallic, iridescent colours of many insects are the direct result of precisely engineered structures. For example, the metallic blues of South American *Morpho* butterflies derive from microscopic, accurately spaced grooves and ridges on the minute scales which cover the wings. The spacing of this surface sculpturing diffracts light in such a way that only blue is reflected; a reflective layer of microfibrils adds a metallic iridescence.

While chitin is truly a wonder substance, having the skeleton on the outside does have its drawbacks: it restricts growth in size. Insects get around this problem by growing in discrete stages, laying down a new cuticle under the existing one and then moulting the latter at a predetermined stage (see the diagram on page 36). Rather than waste a valuable resource, many insects eat their freshly cast cuticle.

The new skeleton is initially soft and flexible, and the insect takes advantage of this by swallowing air or water to expand its volume before the cuticle hardens. After this, extra inner layers (endocuticle) may be laid down. The cuticle is rich in glands which often take the form of complex infoldings. The glands secrete surface waxes, sexual scents and defensive poisons.

Being enclosed in an exoskeleton imposes upper limits on size: the design of the respiratory system (see pages 22–3) is such that, above a certain volume, the network of tracheae becomes inefficient in delivering oxygen to the deeper tissues and voiding them of carbon dioxide. There are mechanical constraints, too: an insect the size of a

ABOVE: *Nothing goes to waste: a fifth-stage nymph of the bush cricket (katydid),* Acrometopa *sp. (Corfu), eats its recently shed skin.*

OPPOSITE: *A nymph of a bush cricket (katydid),* Copiphora rhinoceros, *moults its skin at night in forest (Costa Rica).*

ABOVE: *Arrayed like the overlapping tiles of a roof, the pigmented wing scales of butterflies give them their characteristic colour patterns. In this butterfly, a species of* Morpho *from South America, the scales are without pigments. Instead, the precisely spaced ridges on the scales scatter the light in such a way that only a striking metallic blue is reflected back. This photograph shows only part of a single scale, each of which is smaller than a full stop. It was taken with a scanning electron microscope at a magnification of 440 times.*

LEFT: *A male morpho butterfly,* Morpho pelaides *(French Guyana), rests with his wings open to display his brilliant metallic blue sheen.*

human would require an exoskeleton so thick that there would be no room inside for internal organs!

Nevertheless, insects have an impressive range of sizes. The smallest are smaller than the larger single-celled animals or Protozoa, and the largest are larger than the smaller mammals. The largest insect in terms of bulk is the Hercules beetle, *Dynastes hercules*, of South America, which is two and a half times the weight of a mouse. This is exceptional. The vast majority of insects are very much smaller. Subject to size limits they may be, but, as we shall see, insects are the dominant life-forms in almost all terrestrial habitats: they have cornered the market for tiny to medium-sized animals.

THE NAMING OF PARTS

The body of an adult insect is divided into three main regions: the head, thorax and abdomen.

Head

As with our own bodies, the head contains the brain, eyes and mouthparts. The latter may comprise jaws for biting and chewing, or be modified, tubular structures for sucking or piercing and sucking.

The head also bears the organs of smell. These do not comprise a nose as we know it; instead, insects smell with the antennae, a pair of structures between the eyes. Often called the feelers, the antennae are sensitive to touch as well as smell.

Thorax

This comprises three segments: the prothorax, mesothorax and metathorax. The thorax bears the wings, normally two pairs, and six legs, and much of its bulk is therefore occupied by muscles. It also contains salivary glands additional to those found in the head and the foregut and crop.

Abdomen

In its most primitive state, the abdomen consists of 11 segments, but most modern insects have a reduced number, often due to fusion. The abdomen contains the mid- and hindguts, the insect equivalent of kidneys, the Malpighian tubules, and the sex organs.

OPPOSITE: *The basic divisions of the insect body can become highly modified, as in this common darter dragonfly,* Sympetrum striolatum *(UK), where the head and eyes are massively developed and the abdomen greatly elongated.*

ALIEN ANATOMY: INTERNAL WORKINGS

The insides of insects are very different to ours. To begin with, theirs float in a blood-filled cavity, the haemocoel. Another major difference between them and us is their lack of lungs. And they have a body-length heart and compound, multi-faceted eyes.

The different organ systems are colour coded here for ease of reference.

Digestive system

The insect gut is a simple tube in three sections: foregut, midgut and hindgut. Food passage is lubricated by saliva from glands in the thorax which empty into the foregut. In many, the foregut has a crop in which food may be stored temporarily and crushed. Digestive enzymes are secreted in the midgut and it is here that most nutrients are absorbed. The hindgut regulates excretion of solid wastes and absorbs water from them.

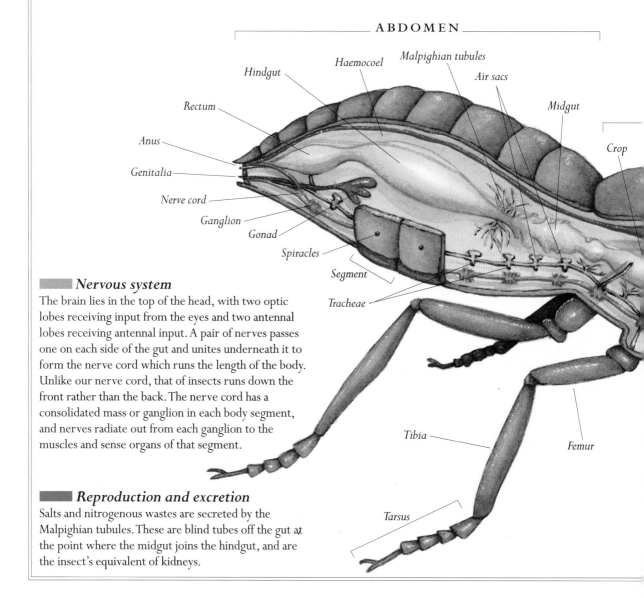

ABDOMEN

Hindgut · Haemocoel · Malpighian tubules · Air sacs · Midgut · Rectum · Anus · Genitalia · Nerve cord · Ganglion · Gonad · Spiracles · Segment · Tracheae · Crop · Tibia · Femur · Tarsus

Nervous system

The brain lies in the top of the head, with two optic lobes receiving input from the eyes and two antennal lobes receiving antennal input. A pair of nerves passes one on each side of the gut and unites underneath it to form the nerve cord which runs the length of the body. Unlike our nerve cord, that of insects runs down the front rather than the back. The nerve cord has a consolidated mass or ganglion in each body segment, and nerves radiate out from each ganglion to the muscles and sense organs of that segment.

Reproduction and excretion

Salts and nitrogenous wastes are secreted by the Malpighian tubules. These are blind tubes off the gut at the point where the midgut joins the hindgut, and are the insect's equivalent of kidneys.

Respiration

Insects do not have lungs; instead, they have a series of special breathing pores (spiracles) along the sides of the body. Each spiracle is controlled by a valve, which opens every five or ten minutes, letting air into a complex network of fine cuticular tubes (tracheae). These divide into ever finer branches (tracheoles) until all tissues receive a supply of oxygen. The finest tracheoles are about one-thousandth of a millimetre in diameter and are so dense that a silkworm caterpillar has about one and a half million of them. This amazing piece of plumbing is shed at every moult, because it is an ingrowth of the cuticle. By keeping the spiracles closed for most of the time, the amount of water vapour lost is minimized and desiccation is avoided.

Circulation

Insects have no real system of blood vessels except for the tubular heart, which runs the full length of the body. The blood system is essentially a cavity, the haemocoel, in which all the internal organs lie bathed in blood. Blood (haemolymph) enters the heart via special valves (ostia) along its length; the heart pumps it forward to the head and thorax, where it then returns to the haemocoel and is directed around the legs and gut. The blood is usually colourless, but may be greeny-yellow; it not only carries nutrients to all parts of the body, but is also the medium by which hormones are carried to their target organs and tissues. The blood also carries special cells which defend against disease organisms, and other cells which repair any structural damage or wounds. Unlike the blood of vertebrates such as ourselves, that of insects does not carry cells involved in respiration.

Vision

Insects have two kinds of eyes: simple eyes, or ocelli, between the larger compound eyes. The latter comprise hundreds to thousands of individual facets, each with its own lens and nerve connection to the brain.

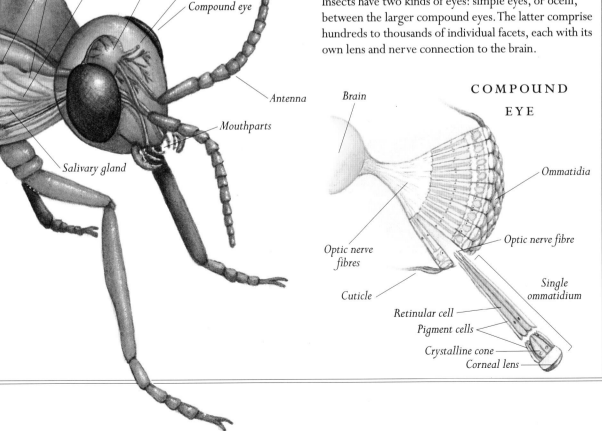

THORAX

Heart Ostia HEAD

Foregut Brain Simple eye

Compound eye

Antenna

Mouthparts

Salivary gland

COMPOUND EYE

Brain

Ommatidia

Optic nerve fibres

Optic nerve fibre

Cuticle

Single ommatidium

Retinular cell

Pigment cells

Crystalline cone

Corneal lens

RIGHT: *A caterpillar of the hawkmoth,* Manduca sexta *(USA). Below are computer-generated simulations of the caterpillar's insides and one of its spiracles.*

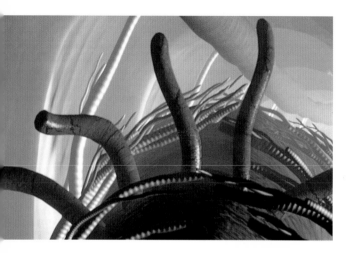

ABOVE: *The inner world of a caterpillar of the hawkmoth. The long red tube is the heart, which pumps blood forwards; the four finger-like processes arising from the central mass of the gut are Malpighian tubules, the insect form of kidney, and the banded tubes are tracheae, the breathing tubes which conduct air from pores or spiracles to all tissues and carbon dioxide to the exterior. All of these organs float in a fluid-filled cavity, the haemocoel.*

ABOVE: *Hugely magnified , a single breathing pore or spiracle. Every body segment has a pair of spiracles, through which air enters the complex system of tracheae or breathing tubes, which permeate the entire body. The aperture of each spiracle is controlled by a valve.*

INSECTS AND EVOLUTION

OPPOSITE: *Dragonflies have their own unique way of minimizing heat absorption. Here, a darter dragonfly,* Trithemis arteriosa *(Kenya), adopts the so-called obelisk posture: it roosts with its long abdomen pointing directly to the sun, thus reducing the surface area exposed to direct solar radiation.*

There are many ways of being an insect. Indeed, there are at least one million ways, for it is a law of nature that each animal species is unique in the ways by which it exploits its environment; each species is finely tuned to respond uniquely to the demands and challenges of being alive. Thus, the basic structural blueprint we have seen is subject to a vast amount of modification and specialization, as is behaviour.

Some of these adaptive responses are bizarre. Consider the Asian moth species, *Lobocraspis griseifusa*, which has apparently given up the habit of drinking nectar from flowers. Instead, it feeds on the tears of buffalo and cattle. And what about another oriental moth, *Calpe eustrigata*, which has taken a further step and uses its sucking mouthparts to pierce the skin of mammals and drink their blood? Ecologically, it has become a mosquito.

Insects have evolved ways of coping with extremes of temperature. There are distant relatives of crickets, called rock crawlers (grylloblattids), which live in the snowfields of high mountains, often in ice caves. Restricted to western North America and the Himalayas, they feed on windborne insects which have succumbed to hypothermia. These cold-hardy insects produce their own anti-freeze, glycerol, which prevents ice crystals forming in their body fluids, enabling them to be active at low temperatures which would be lethal to other animals. Many insects, including the more familiar ladybirds (ladybugs), have this facility.

At the other extreme are the larvae of the African midge, *Polypedilum vanderplanckii*. They live in small temporary pools subject to drying out, and can survive total desiccation, for years if necessary. When drenched in water, they revive quickly.

BELOW: *Seven-spot ladybirds,* Coccinella septempunctata *(UK), hibernate in snow. Like many other insects, these ladybirds have their own anti-freeze which prevents their body fluids from freezing.*

Ultra-specialization of this kind is common. Less common is the kind of extreme flexibility seen in a little scuttle fly, *Megaselia scalaris*. The larvae feed on a wide range of rotting organic matter, but have developed quite happily on shoe polish, emulsion paint and human cadavers pickled in formalin. Almost out of bravado, it seems, they have also been found living in the lungs of Japanese university students.

Insects living in extreme deserts need to avoid desiccation and the harmful glare of ultra-violet radiation. This darkling beetle, Cauricara eburnea *(Namibia), has reflective white wing cases which also make it inconspicuous among the quartzite gravel.*

This book deals with many behavioural and structural adaptations of insects. How can we account for this recurrent theme of diversity through specialization? Modern biology explains it by invoking natural selection, a much misunderstood process.

The concept of natural selection originated with Charles Darwin, in his book *The Origin of Species*, published in 1859. Rather enigmatically, Darwin defined natural selection as the 'survival of the fittest'. Many people thought that by 'fittest', he referred to physical strength or fitness in the athletic sense of the word. In fact, he meant that in a population of the same species, containing much inherent variation, some individuals would be better fitted than others to cope with the demands of the environment and with competition with other organisms. Those individuals which were more efficient in what Darwin called the struggle for existence would, on average, produce more offspring than less efficient ones. Assuming that the superior qualities were inherited, then, in time, the proportion of more efficient individuals would increase in the population. As he explained in his Introduction to *The Origin of Species*:

> As many more individuals of each species are born than can possibly survive; and as, consequently, there is a frequently recurring struggle for existence, it follows that any being, if it vary however slightly in any manner profitable to itself, under the complex and sometimes varying conditions of life, will have a better chance of surviving, and thus be *naturally selected*.

In the fourth edition of his book, published in 1869, Darwin added a passage to explain what natural selection was *not*, for his critics had largely misunderstood him. Natural selection was not the cause of variability within a species, nor was it a creative force acting as an agent for the deity. Some people had wrongly assumed that by natural selection, Darwin implied a conscious choice on the part of animals. If his critics had read him more carefully, they would not have had these difficulties.

Nevertheless, Darwin's theory was not entirely satisfying: there was something missing. His whole case rested on the recurrence of individual variation in successive generations. While this variation is an observable fact — children of the same human parents can differ in eye colour, hair texture and stature — the biology of the day offered no mechanism of heredity which could explain its existence. Indeed, Darwin and his contemporaries held a view of heredity which was incompatible with the theory of natural selection. They believed that in sexually reproducing species, each offspring represented a blend of traits inherited from the parents. Darwin soon realized that if blending inheritance took place, then, in time, populations would become uniform in all characteristics. The problem of heredity and individual variation was to puzzle Darwin for the rest of his life.

It is ironic, therefore, that research which provided the very explanation he required was begun in 1856 and published in 1866, the very decade that saw the first four editions of Darwin's *Origin of Species*.

A Moravian monk, Gregor Mendel, working in the garden of the Augustinian monastery in Brno, then in Austria, studied the inheritance of certain characteristics in the garden pea. By a series of elegantly designed breeding experiments, he showed that individual traits such as the colour and texture of the seed are inherited by means of discrete 'factors' which are segregated in the sex cells and passed from one generation to the next. In plants, these sex cells are the pollen grains (male) and the ovules (female), which correspond to the sperm and eggs in animals. Collectively, the sex cells are called gametes.

The 'hereditary factors' were later christened genes and shown by subsequent researchers to be material entities arranged rather like the beads of a necklace along threads called chromosomes. These are found

LEFT: *Long legs in this tiger beetle,* Cicindela *sp. (Florida), keep the body out of contact with the burning hot sand.*

OVERLEAF: *Protective resemblance to a mossy twig is part of the defensive repertoire of this rainforest bush cricket (katydid),* Championica *sp. (Costa Rica).*

in the nucleus of each body cell. We now know that a chromosome comprises a pair of threads, one from each of the parents. The genes contained therein encode all the hereditary or genetic information which is passed from one generation to the next.

The number of chromosomes in animal and plant cells is characteristic for each species. Thus, we have 46 chromosomes and the housefly has 12. The chromosome number is also constant from one generation to another. This would appear to create a problem: when an egg is fertilized, the genetic material from the two parents combines to form the new individual, thus apparently doubling the number of chromosomes. If this happened in each generation, then the amount of genetic material would increase geometrically with time.

In fact, the cells which will ultimately become sperm or eggs undergo a special kind of division (meiosis) in which the amount of genetic material is halved: the members of each pair of chromosomes become separated, one strand going into one of the cells resulting from division, the second going into the other one. Thus the sperm or egg has

EGGS: THE FIRST SURVIVAL CAPSULES

Insect eggs are protected by a shell of the wonder substance, chitin. There is an astonishing variety in egg design, a variety that almost matches that of adult insects themselves.

Although insects are masters of miniaturization, paradoxically their eggs are among the largest of all animal eggs. They are dwarfed only by those of the amphibia, reptiles and birds. The smallest of insect eggs is many thousands of times larger than a human egg.

Insects lay eggs in a variety of places, and the design of an egg is matched to its habitat. Thus, the eggs of water bugs have a shell with an intricate microstructure called a plastron, which enables the egg to breathe under water. Indeed, many eggs have the most elegant of micro-sculpturing. Butterflies lay eggs with a pattern of strengthening ribs and pockets, giving them the appearance of miniature hand grenades.

Whatever the fine details of structure, an eggshell has one major function: to protect the developing embryo from extremes of temperature and humidity.

LEFT: *Taken with a scanning electron microscope magnifying 80 times, this picture shows an egg of a butterfly with its beautiful microscopic sculpturing typical of many insect eggs.*

half the normal amount of genetic material and is said to be haploid. Normal cells, with the full complement of chromosomes, are diploid.

During this reduction division, maternal and paternal chromosomes exchange genes. Thus in the process leading to sperm and egg production, combinations of genes are reshuffled, so that each resultant sperm or egg has a unique genetic profile: no two sperm or eggs from the same parent have an identical complement of genes. And herein lies part of the answer to Darwin's dilemma: how can one account for the regular occurrence of variation between the individuals of a species?

The rest of the answer lies in sex. When a sperm fertilizes an egg, the nucleus of one fuses with the other, so that each chromosome finds its counterpart from the opposite sex and the normal, diploid, number of chromosomes is restored.

The whole process of courtship and mating in animals, and pollination in plants, is geared to bring about the union of chromosomes from the opposite sexes. Thus, each offspring receives exactly half of its genetic information, the blueprint for development and survival, from

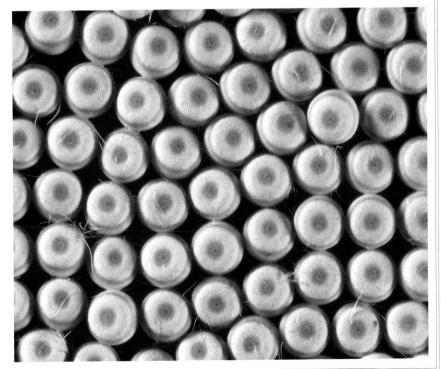

RIGHT: *An egg mass of the vapourer moth,* Orgyia antiqua *(UK). The wingless female of this species remains on her cocoon after emergence, mates, lays her eggs there and dies soon afterwards.*

LEFT: *Also hugely magnified (60 times using a scanning electron microscope), an end-on view of an egg of a water bug, the so-called water scorpion,* Nepa cineraria. *This picture shows the seven filaments which together form a plastron or special gill through which the egg obtains oxygen from the water.*

The pale form of the peppered moth, Biston betularia *(UK), well camouflaged while roosting on its normal background of lichen-covered bark.*

each parent. This results in a novel combination of genes in each generation and is the basis of the uniqueness of the individual. With the exception of identical twins, derived from a divided, fertilized egg, no two offspring from the same parents are genetically identical. This is true of all sexually reproducing organisms, including insects and people.

Mendel's work complements Darwin's theory because it demonstrates the inheritance of discrete factors or genes and provides an explanation of the origin of variations on which natural selection acts.

The process of natural selection has now been amply demonstrated by observation and experiment, but what exactly *is* natural selection and how does it work?

One of the most potent experimental proofs of natural selection began long before Darwin published *The Origin of Species*. It took place not in the laboratory, but in the increasingly polluted countryside of Victorian England; and the experimenter was not a white-coated scientist, but, inadvertently, the Industrial Revolution.

The common peppered moth, *Biston betularia*, is a pale species, with its wing pattern comprising a fine speckling of black spots and bands on a white background. In 1848, moth hunters in the Manchester area noticed the appearance of a black or melanic form of *B. betularia*, which they aptly named as *carbonaria*. Seven years later, this had increased in frequency until 98 per cent of some populations consisted of the melanic form *carbonaria*. The peppered moth breeds only once a year, so this change was extremely rapid.

ABOVE: *Poorly camouflaged on pale lichen-covered tree trunks, the black form of the peppered moth,* Biston betularia, *form* carbonaria, *was easy prey to birds and was rare until industrial pollution killed lichens in nineteenth-century England.*

B. betularia flies by night and, by day, roosts in shaded spots, such as on the underside of branches, or just below the point where a branch joins the tree trunk. The moth roosts with its wings spread out. In unpolluted areas, trees tend to be covered with rough-textured pale grey lichens. Against this background, *B. betularia* is well camouflaged and protected from predation by birds.

Lichens are very sensitive to airborne pollution and soon disappeared from industrial areas and countryside downwind of them. The trees lost their lichen covering and became black; against this background, the normal, pale, form of *B. betularia* was very conspicuous and easy prey to birds. Prior to the Industrial Revolution, the black form, *carbonaria*, was a very rare mutant, so rare, in fact, that moth collectors had never found it. Its rarity was maintained by birds, which found *carbonaria* very easy to pick out on the pale, lichen-covered tree branches.

In other words, the melanic *carbonaria* was at a selective disadvantage in unpolluted areas, and insectivorous birds were the selective agents; it was rare because selective pressure against it was intense.

With the advent of the Industrial Revolution, the tables were turned; *carbonaria* suddenly enjoyed a selective advantage and the normal form was at a disadvantage because it was now conspicuous against the blackened, lichen-free trees. The birds, as selective agents, did not consciously select any particular colour pattern of the moth: they simply caught those moths which they saw.

The black colour of *carbonaria* is controlled by a single gene. Natural

TWO WAYS OF GROWING UP

Insects can be divided into two major groups according to how they grow and develop. In the more primitive insects, the egg hatches to produce a larva or nymph which resembles a miniature version of the adult, except that there are no wings and the sex glands are undeveloped.

Development is in several stages, each punctuated by a moulting of the cuticle. Growth in size occurs while the new cuticle is still soft. With each successive moult, more adult characteristics appear. Insects with this gradual type of development are said to have an incomplete metamorphosis; they are called 'exopterygotes' because their wings develop externally. The immature stages usually live in habitats similar to those of the adults and share much the same kind of diet. Familiar insects with this pattern of development are cockroaches, grasshoppers and earwigs.

The more advanced insects have a complete metamorphosis. That is, the egg hatches into a larva which bears no resemblance to the adult and very often differs from it in diet and habitat. Such insects are called 'endopterygotes' because their wings develop internally. The larva undergoes a series of moults as it grows and then becomes a pupa. During the pupal stage, almost all larval tissues are broken down and reassembled into the adult form; only the nervous system and part of the gut remain relatively unchanged.

Because it is inactive, the pupa is vulnerable, so the last larval stage usually chooses a safe, sheltered spot in which to pupate. The caterpillars (larvae) of most moths spin a tough silk cocoon for added protection.

Familiar insects with this kind of development include moths, butterflies, bees and wasps. (See page 39 for a complete listing of the major groups of insects.)

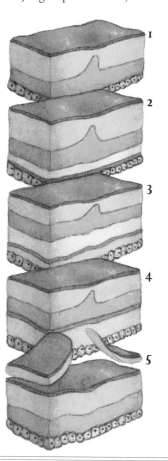

LEFT: *An unnamed cicada nymph moults at night in temperate forest, South Africa. This is a vulnerable time, so moulting at night reduces the risks of predation.*

RIGHT: *Moulting is a complex process, under hormonal control. The cuticle has four layers (1). First, old, unhardened endocuticle is broken down and reabsorbed (1, 2) and then a rather wrinkled new layer of epicuticle is laid down (3), the wrinkles allowing for later expansion under a layer of moulting fluid (4). Bulking protein and chitin are then laid down below the new epicuticle (3, 4). When this is complete, the external, older cuticle splits along distinct lines of weakness (5) and the insect wriggles out of its old skeleton.*

COMPLETE METAMORPHOSIS: THE BLACK SWALLOWTAIL BUTTERFLY

1 *A first-stage caterpillar of* Papilio polyxenes *(USA), with egg. The caterpillar mimics a bird dropping.*

2 *An older caterpillar feeding on its special foodplant, dill.*

3 *A caterpillar moulting its cuticle.*

4 *About to pupate, this caterpillar suspends itself in a girdle of two silk threads.*

5 *The fully formed pupa suspended by silk secreted by the last caterpillar stage. Larval tissues are broken down and re-formed into adult structures.*

7 *...expands its wings by pumping blood into its network of veins.*

6 *The new adult begins to break its way out of the pupal case and...*

8 *Yet to make its first flight, the newly emerged adult black swallowtail rests with fully expanded wings folded over its abdomen, showing the distinctive pattern of the undersides of the wings.*

selection, in the form of predation by birds, increased the frequency of this gene in populations living in polluted areas. When smoke abatement policies began to take effect in the industrial areas of northern England, lichens reappeared on trees and the frequency of normal, pale-coloured *Biston betularia* began to increase. Thus, in some circumstances, the effects of natural selection can be reversed.

We can now state Darwin's theory more precisely: evolution is the process by which natural selection alters the frequency of genes in populations, resulting in structural, behavioural and physiological change.

Our example of natural selection in action is a very simple one: it involves selection acting, via a single agent, on a single facet of an insect's life. The struggle for existence, however, is fought on a broad front. Selection operates, via many different environmental agents and influences, on not only appearance, but all the complexities of behaviour and structure and the usually invisible processes of development and physiology. In this way, all the finely tuned, highly evolved adaptations of insects and the huge diversity of their species came into being, honed in the laboratory of the living world.

But selection is not all about innovation: it can be conservative, too. Any drastic deviation from, say, basic physiological functions is likely to be detrimental; if selection brings about the survival of the fittest, it also ensures the survival of the ordinary.

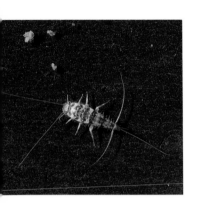

A firebrat, a primitive wingless insect, Thermobia domestica *(UK), so called because it can survive hot, dry habitats. It is often found living in crevices behind the firebricks in fireplaces and bakers' ovens.*

SUCCESS IN DIVERSITY

The insect class, Insecta, is divided into two sub-classes, the Apterygota (wingless) and the Pterygota (winged). Some of the orders of insects within the sub-classes have incomplete metamorphosis, while others have complete metamorphosis. The orders are identified in the table opposite. The total given here is, of course, a gross underestimate. It is an indication of the number of insect species which have been formally described. About 7000 new species are described each year, especially in beetles, flies and parasitic wasps. Sadly, this figure may now be exceeded by the annual extinction of undescribed species resulting from the destruction of habitats, especially tropical forests.

Recent estimates of the likely total number of insect species are based on representative samples collected on tropical trees and range from 15 to 30 million.

THE CLASSIFICATION OF INSECTS

Sub-class: Apterygota (wingless insects)

Order	Common name	No. of species
✳ Archaeognatha	—	250
✳ Thysanura	Bristletails	330

Sub-class: Pterygota (winged insects)

Order	Common name	No. of species
✳ Odonata	Dragonflies, damselflies	5 000
✳ Ephemeroptera	Mayflies	2 000
✳ Blattodea	Cockroaches	3 500
✳ Isoptera	Termites	2 230
✳ Mantodea	Praying mantids	1 800
✳ Zoraptera	—	22
✳ Dermaptera	Earwigs	1 200
✳ Grylloblatodea	Rock crawlers	20
✳ Plecoptera	Stoneflies	3 000
✳ Orthoptera	Crickets, grasshoppers, locusts	20 000
✳ Phasmatodea	Stick insects, walking leaves	2 500
✳ Embioptera	Webspinners	200
✳ Psocoptera	Booklice, barklice	3 000
✳ Phthiraptera	Parasitic lice	3 150
✳ Hemiptera	True bugs	67 500
✳ Thysanoptera	Thrips, thunderflies	5 000
✳ Megaloptera	Alderflies, dobsonflies, fishflies	300
✳ Neuroptera	Lacewings, ant lions	5 000
✳ Coleoptera	Beetles	300 000
✳ Strepsiptera	Stylops, twisted-winged insects	350
✳ Diptera	True, 2-winged flies	250 000
✳ Trichoptera	Caddisflies	7 000
✳ Lepidoptera	Butterflies, moths	150 000
✳ Hymenoptera	Sawflies, ichneumons, chalcids, wasps, ants, bees	200 000
Total:		**1 033 352**

✳ Orders with incomplete metamorphosis

✳ Orders with complete metamorphosis

2

ULTIMATE ROBOTS

Making sense of the world

*The long antennae of this female bush cricket
(katydid), Acrometopa sp. (Corfu), enable
it to probe cavities and under leaves for food.*

LIKE US, INSECTS SEE, taste, smell and feel. Many can hear and all sense vibrations. But they can do much more: they have their own on-board clock, magnetic compass and gyroscopes.

Even where they share senses with us, they differ profoundly in the way their sense organs work. And the ways in which information from these sensors are processed are the envy of all computer scientists.

As the true miracles of miniaturization, insects compress all this processing power into a tiny brain, an on-board, preprogrammed computer. According to species, this may consist of anything from only a few thousand to slightly more than a million cells. A human brain has hundreds of billions of cells. A computer with the processing power of an insect brain, assuming we could build one, would be the size of a small tower block, and maybe even larger than this if we include the necessary cooling system.

VISION

Up to 80 per cent of the insect brain processes information from the eyes and antennae. This is not surprising, because in many insects, especially flies and dragonflies, the eyes are enormous and occupy most of the area of the head.

Insects have two kinds of eye: simple eyes (ocelli) and a pair of compound eyes. There are usually three simple eyes, arranged in a triangle which may be on the top of the head, between the compound eyes or in front of them.

Each simple eye has a curved, transparent cuticular lens. Simple eyes do not form an image; instead, they are sensitive to low levels of light and subtle changes in light intensity, and enhance the detection of light by the compound eyes. They are also sensitive to the changes in light intensity which take place during the course of the day. This is presumably linked to the insect's sense of time.

The compound eyes are the actual organs of vision, which produce an image of the world. However, they are very different to our eyes. A compound eye comprises thousands of tiny hexagonal units called ommatidia. Each has a cuticular lens which directs light into a long light guide beneath it. The light strikes light-sensitive nerve cells and each ommatidium generates its own image in the brain.

The image, though, is very different from ours. An insect cannot

form as detailed or highly resolved an image as we can. Instead, the compound eye as a whole is very sensitive to contrasts, patterns and shape. Moreover, because each ommatidium has such a narrow field of vision, the insect eye is extremely sensitive to movement: a moving object triggers a split-second image in one ommatidium then stimulates adjacent ones and so on. The faster an object moves across an insect's visual field, the more clearly it is registered. Thus, for an insect in flight, the faster the object, the closer it is.

Apart from anything else, then, the compound eye is a remarkably sensitive movement and distance detector, which is just what a flying insect needs. When did you last manage to catch a fly in your hand?

A stationary insect is just as sensitive to movement and can react in an instant, with flies, some butterflies and some kinds of bee being particularly quick off the mark. Only the lightning tongue of a chameleon is a match for these insects.

The human eye fuses a flickering image into a continuous one at 15 frames a second. Insect eyes see individual images at 100 frames per second. Fast-flying insects such as flies have evolved this system in order to cope with high speed flight through structurally complex environments, in situations where no human pilot could cope.

BELOW: *Magnified 270 times, just a few of the thousands of hexagonal facets which make up the surface of a fly's compound eye (scanning electron micrograph).*

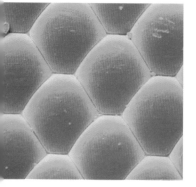

RIGHT: *Catching insect prey on the wing is the forte of dragonflies, such as this* Orthetrum julia *(Kenya), so huge, multi-faceted eyes are a vital asset.*

Flying insects have special 'edge' detectors in the brain: these are sensitive to vertical edges in the visual field of the flight path. If they are tilted from the vertical, the insect corrects its attitude until they register as vertical again. Thus, the insect can constantly correct its in-flight attitude, just like the latest fly-by-wire passenger aircraft. Insects, though, were doing this long before the dinosaurs appeared.

In many insects, the visual fields of the two compound eyes overlap, so there is an area of stereoscopic vision in front. Very often this stereo-vision is found in insects such as dragonflies, praying mantids and horse-flies, which have huge eyes with all-round vision. This means that the on-board computer can process different kinds of visual information at the same time. However, because the insect eye does not resolve such detailed images as ours, the brain is not overloaded with irrelevant information.

Another visual feat of insects is their ability to detect the plane of polarized light. The atmosphere polarizes the sun's rays, so that they vibrate in a certain direction. Being able to detect this enables insects to use the sun as a navigational beacon, even in cloudy weather, when the sun is not directly visible. This is of particular importance to migrating insects and to nesting species such as wasps, ants and bees, which have to be able to find their way back to the nest.

Many insects have colour vision. They see colours much as we do, but their sensitivity is shifted to the blue end of the spectrum: they can detect ultra-violet light, but most are virtually blind to the red end of the spectrum. As we shall see, this sensitivity of insects to ultra-violet is exploited by many plants.

A SENSE OF SMELL AND TASTE

Insects have a highly sensitive sense of smell. Using the feelers or antennae, the principal organ of smell, a male moth may detect the scent of a female from a distance of several miles; flesh flies and carrion beetles can detect rotting bodies over similar distances. And, as we shall see, many insects use scent as a means of communication, sometimes in very complex ways. The sensors of the antennae are geared to detect airborne molecules.

Although insects may be very good at detecting the tiniest traces of scents, their repertoire of scent recognition is rather more limited than

OPPOSITE: *Branched antennae increase the surface area of reception and therefore enhance the sense of smell in this praying mantis, Vates sp. (Trinidad).*

FEATHERY ANTENNAE

As in all insect sense organs, those of smell are highly modified cuticular structures. The basic sensory unit of the antenna is a special microscopic hair or peg-like structure called a sensillum (see diagram right). This has many tiny pores all over its surface varying from 10- to 15-thousandths of a millimetre in diameter. Behind the entrance of each pore is a tiny chamber lined with a membrane and called the pore kettle. The membrane is itself perforated with many tiny pores, each leading via an ultra-microscopic tube to a sensitive, electrically charged membrane connected to multi-branched nerve fibres.

An insect's sensilla operate first by capturing airborne molecules in the pore kettles; these travel via the micro-tubes to the electrically polarized membrane at the far end, and trigger nerve impulses to the brain. It seems the molecule momentarily depolarizes the membrane and this stimulates a nerve impulse.

BELOW: *Magnified 120 times, thousands of sensory hairs on the branched, feathery antennae of a male moth trawl the air for scent molecules. This dense array of sensors is a super-efficient way of detecting scent-emitting females over long distances (scanning electron micrograph).*

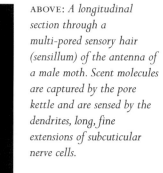

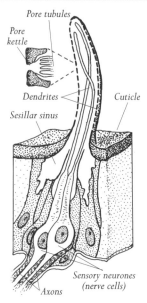

ABOVE: *A longitudinal section through a multi-pored sensory hair (sensillum) of the antenna of a male moth. Scent molecules are captured by the pore kettle and are sensed by the dendrites, long, fine extensions of subcuticular nerve cells.*

LEFT: *The multi-branched antennae of this male emperor moth, Rothschildia sp. (Costa Rica), greatly increase the receptive area of these ultra-sensitive organs of smell, enabling him to detect the faintest traces of female scents.*

The pattern of depolarizations is characteristic of the molecules involved. In this way, a male moth can recognize a specific scent, say that of a sexually receptive female, or a bee can identify the characteristic scent of a flower it has learned is a rich source of pollen or nectar.

With many thousands of sensillae of this kind on each antenna, it is easy to understand just how sensitive is the insect's sense of smell. Many different kinds of insect have independently evolved a neat way of enhancing this sensitivity even further: they increase the surface area of reception by having branched antennae, which act as efficient molecular sieves, trawling the air for scent molecules.

This kind of branched or pectinate antenna is particularly well developed in many male moths. In the male silk moth, *Bombyx mori*, for example, each antenna has about 17 000 sensillae. These respond to the species-specific sexual scent or pheromone emitted by female silk moths.

Each sensillum has about 3000 pores, so each moth has a total of 102 million pores. It has been calculated that some species of moth with pectinate antennae of this sort capture about a third of all pheromone molecules which pass over them.

With such a massive array of sensors, the antennae need to capture only a few molecules of pheromone in order to elicit a nerve impulse; fewer than 100 molecules are needed to trigger a behavioural response and drive the male to start searching for the calling female. And she may be several miles away.

Pheromones are, in any case, released in very small quantities, and antennae are very selective: of the many different odours in the environment, antennae are highly sensitive to the relatively few scents which are relevant to the behaviour of a particular insect.

ABOVE: *Branched, feathery antennae are not restricted to male moths. Many other male insects have branched antennae, such as this cockchafer,* Melolontha melolontha *(UK).*

RIGHT: *Another insect to have independently arrived at this device to increase the surface area of sensors is this praying mantis,* Einpusa pennata *(France).*

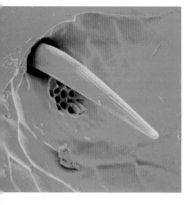

ours: they respond only to a narrow range of scents which are relevant to their behaviour, yet another way of preventing the on-board computer from being overloaded with irrelevant information.

Sensors of taste are found on the mouthparts. They are also found on the tarsal segments of the legs, so, in effect, insects taste with their feet. When a butterfly's tarsi contact traces of nectar sugars at a flower, this stimulates the uncoiling of the long proboscis in readiness for feeding.

In many insects, taste sensors are also found near the tip of the female's egg-laying tube or ovipositor. This enables the female to identify appropriate egg-laying sites, such as the leaves of specific plants or dead wood of a particular age and stage of decomposition.

The structure of the sensors is similar to that of scent detectors, but is adapted for dealing with chemicals in solution rather than airborne molecules.

TOUCH

Because insects are encased in an armour-plated cuticle, one might be forgiven for thinking that a sense of touch is relatively unimportant to them. They are, however, endowed with a variety of touch receptors. These are distributed all over the outer surface of the body, with particular concentrations at limb joints, the joints between body segments, and in the tarsal segments which come into contact with whatever surface the insect happens to be on.

Most touch receptors work by means of the deformation of a membrane which is connected to a nerve fibre. The commonest form has a hair (seta) which grows out of a shallow pit in the cuticle. Like the cuticle, the hair is made of chitin; it is produced by a single cell under the pit. The base of the hair is fused with a flexible membrane stretched across the pit.

When the insect touches an object with the hair, or if something touches the hair, it bends and deforms the membrane. This sends impulses down the nerve attached to the membrane and the hair base. The frequency of nerve impulses is directly related to the extent of the deformation.

With many touch receptors of this type being stimulated at the same time, a walking insect, for example, can feel the texture of the surface it is walking on.

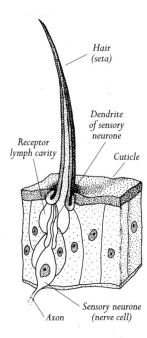

Hair
(seta)

Dendrite
of sensory
neurone

Receptor
lymph cavity

Cuticle

Axon

Sensory neurone
(nerve cell)

ABOVE: *A section through a sensory hair (seta) which is the basis of the sense of touch in insects.*

Near the base of each antenna, there is a modified form of touch receptor. This is called Johnston's organ and it is a flight speed indicator: the greater the antennal bases are deformed by the pressure of flowing air, the greater the sense of speed perceived.

Worker honeybees have an additional way of assessing the speed of flight. They have long hairs between the facets of the eyes; these form a dense array of receptors and, as the bee flies, the hairs are bent by the air stream flowing over them. Each hair has its own nerve at its base and, the greater the deformation of the hairs, the greater the airspeed perceived by the bee.

Special touch receptors are also sensitive to vibrations transmitted through whatever surface the insect is on. Thus, both sexes of many species of planthoppers produce a low-frequency song which transmits as vibrations through plant stems and leaves.

Insect touch receptors are not only geared to dealing with input from the outside world. Many special receptors, called proprioceptors, are dedicated to telling the insect about itself, especially where its movable body parts are relative to each other.

Where, say, two segments of the abdomen or two leg parts articulate, on one of them there is an array of sensory hairs which come into contact with the other part when it moves relative to it. Again, the extent of deflection of the hairs and their basal membrane is important. In this case, the greater the deflection, the greater the relative movement between the two body parts.

Consider an active insect which is running along the ground, using its antennae to feel and smell its way around: it is a mass of moving, jointed parts. The proprioceptors distributed throughout the body surface give the insect an instant fix on where all its parts are relative to one another.

HEARING

The perception of sound is the perception of airborne vibrations. Adult humans can detect sounds in a rather limited range of frequencies: from 20 to 20 000Hz – 1 hertz (Hz) is a frequency of one cycle per second. The range of sounds perceived by insects as a whole is from 1 to 100 000Hz, though each insect species has a much narrower range, related to its own functional needs.

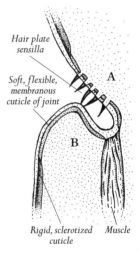

BELOW: *Section through the articulation between two body parts of an insect, to show how the relative movement of adjacent parts is detected. Hairs of the plate sensilla of part A are deformed when part B moves relative to them. Nerve impulses from this sense organ (proprioceptor) signal the relative positions of A and B.*

Hair plate sensilla

Soft, flexible, membranous cuticle of joint

A

B

Rigid, sclerotized cuticle   Muscle

OVERLEAF: *Extremely long antennae enable this scavenging cricket, Phaephilacris sp. (Kenya), probe under leaf litter and under bark for food.*

HEARING AIDS

Hearing in many insects involves a special receptor, the tympanum, which is sensitive to airborne vibrations. This tympanum is a membrane which vibrates in response to incoming sound. It is attached to clusters of specialized proprioceptor cells, which detect the deformations in the membrane. These cells are themselves connected to the auditory nerve, which translates the vibrations into nerve impulses which are conducted to the brain.

We can call the tympanum and its associated structures the insect ear. The exact position of the ears in the body depends on the insects concerned:

* Front legs: bush crickets (katydids), mole crickets, crickets.
* Thorax between hind legs: praying mantids.
* Wings: lacewings, some moths.
* Abdomen: grasshoppers, cicadas, some moths.

The fact that ears occur in such widely differing parts of the body in different insects is an indication that they have evolved independently many times.

In bush crickets, the hearing system is remarkably complex (see diagram below). Two tympanic membranes lie in a cavity at the base of the tibiae of the front legs. Internal to each membrane is a modified breathing tube (trachea), which runs up the centre of

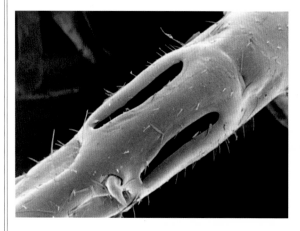

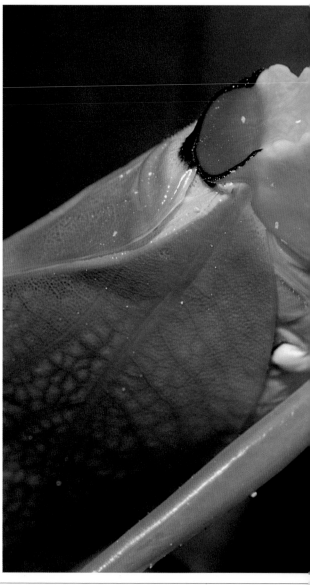

ABOVE: *Magnified 35 times, a pair of slits on the front leg of a bush cricket (katydid) are part of the insect's complex ear structure (scanning electron micrograph).*

BELOW: *A section through the prothorax and front legs of a bush cricket (katydid), showing those parts of the respiratory system modified for the detection of sound.*

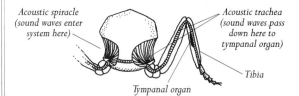

Acoustic spiracle (sound waves enter system here)

Acoustic trachea (sound waves pass down here to tympanal organ)

Tibia

Tympanal organ

the leg, ending in an enlarged and modified breathing pore (spiracle) in the prothorax.

Both tracheae and spiracles are modified in the sense that they are not connected to the rest of the system of tracheae and spiracles which make up the respiratory system. Instead, the spiracle, called the acoustic spiracle, acts as a receiver of sound waves; from the spiracle, sound waves pass down the column of air in the trachea and vibrate the tympanic membranes. Just behind the acoustic spiracle, the trachea is swollen and acts as an amplifier as the sound waves pass through it.

The cavity in the leg which contains the two membranes opens to the outside via two slits. It has been suggested that the two slits act as sound guides and may be involved in directional hearing.

LEFT: *The swelling with a slit at the base of the front tibiae of this bush cricket (katydid),* Stilpnochlora incisa *(Peru), contains the tympanic membranes which translate incoming sound waves into patterns of sound perceived by the brain.*

For example, the hearing range of female grasshoppers approximates to the range of sounds made by singing males of their own species. The male of each species has its own specific song, so females of other species, even closely related ones, are effectively deaf to them. The same is probably true of other insects, such as female cicadas, which detect mates by species-specific sounds emitted by males.

INTEGRATION: PUTTING IT ALL TOGETHER

An active insect, going about its business, processes all the input from its different sense organs. With such a wide range of sensory input, an insect has, at the very least, a profound sense of where it is in space.

The task of the brain is to process and integrate this information, so that the appropriate, preprogrammed patterns of behaviour are triggered. A good example is a dragonfly, hunting for insect prey on the wing. As it flies, its huge eyes constantly scan the forward visual field for prey. At the same time, it continuously monitors its airspeed, so that it 'knows' if it has to decelerate to swoop on a slower insect or if it has to

Dragonflies are noted aerial acrobats, so the fact that this two-striped forceptail, Aphylla williamsi (USA), has caught and is eating another hawker dragonfly is a tribute to its finely tuned sensory co-ordination.

accelerate to bear down on a faster one. While all this is going on, the dragonfly also monitors and adjusts its attitude using its on-board gyroscope: sensory hairs at the back of the head which impinge on the thorax immediately behind it detect alterations in the relative positions of head and thorax.

Having locked on to a flying insect, say a small moth or a caddisfly, the dragonfly opens its spiny, dangling legs to form an aerial trawl and grasp the prey. This is a high level of co-ordination and is the match of any mammal.

Many insects can store received information: their memory is well-developed. This is particularly true of nesting insects.

A female solitary wasp, for example, may excavate a nest burrow in the soil. When she has finished her digging, she makes some short, loop-ing or figure-of-eight flights just above her nest entrance. She is mem-orizing visual cues in the immediate neighbourhood of her nest. These may be some pebbles, a twig and some clumps of grass.

The female gradually increases the sizes of her loops and figures-of-eight: she is memorizing more distant cues, such as a clump of trees, a church steeple and a mountain peak on the horizon.

Now she flies off in search of some prey with which to store her brood cells. The prey might be caterpillars; she seeks out a suitable source, say a small group of shrubs, a quarter of a mile from her nest.

As she flies towards this, she uses the position of the sun as a navi-gational beacon. It does not matter that it is a cloudy day and that the sun is periodically obscured: she monitors the plane of polarized light and thus can still use the sun.

She arrives at the shrubs and spends some time searching for a cater-pillar. Eventually, she finds one, paralyses it with her sting and then sets off on her return journey, carrying the prey with her legs and holding on to it with her jaws.

She has memorized her position and route relative to the sun's pos-ition. The sun, however, has an annoying habit of moving across the sky. This does not faze our wasp. She has an in-built clock, which enables her to compensate for the sun's changed position. So, having made this adjustment, she can still use the sun's position as one of the navigational cues to guide her back to the nest. She also uses her visual memory of the distant, horizon landmarks and then homes in to the nest itself, using the closer cues. While she is flying back to her nest, using this

DANCING THE GOOD NEWS

The most highly sophisticated integration of perceived and memorized information is found in the western honeybee, *Apis mellifera*: recently returned workers are able to communicate the direction, distance and quality of food sources to their nest-mates and thus recruit more foragers.

Our understanding of how this communication works is due to the Austrian scientist, Karl Von Frisch, in some of the most elegant experiments ever conducted by an animal behaviourist.

It was first noticed that worker honeybees could communicate the whereabouts of a food source when a marked bee was provided with an artificial source of honey-solution. Although the bee was prevented from leaving the hive, other workers soon began to exploit the food. Clearly, some form of communication had occurred.

Using a glass-sided observation hive, Von Frisch observed that a returning forager often performed a ritualized series of movements on the honeycomb, which attracted the attention of other workers. He called these movements 'dances'. After many painstaking observations and experiments, using individually marked bees and artificial food sources of varying quality and at different distances from the hive, Von Frisch finally translated the dance language of the honeybee. Subsequent researchers added to this understanding.

A forager returned from a food source within 25m (80ft) of the hive performs the round dance – **(1)** in the diagram opposite. This comprises a series of circular runs, with regular changes of direction. A dancing worker attracts and holds the attention of a group of workers called followers. They constantly touch her with their antennae and taste nectar she regurgitates from time to time. The frequency of direction changes in the round dance, together with the general vigour of its performance, indicates the quality of the food,

A worker honeybee, Apis mellifera *(UK), has found a source of pollen and nectar. Soon she will be back at the hive, dancing the good news.*

that is, its calorific value.

The round dance does not convey the direction of the food source. Because this is within 25m of the hive, workers recruited to exploit it can find it quickly enough by flying away from the hive in ever-increasing circles.

For a food source greater than 100m (330ft) from the hive, a returned forager performs the waggle dance **(2)**. This is a flattened figure-of-eight; on the straight run between the two semi-circles making up the figure, she waggles her abdomen very rapidly from side to side and buzzes rapidly. The length of the straight run and the number of waggles in it indicate the distance of the food source from the hive. The attending followers measure the length of the straight run by the number of cells of the comb she passes over. It seems that distance is expressed in terms of the energy required to get there. The tempo of the dance, and the number of times she repeats it, together with high frequency buzzes of 250Hz, are indications of the quality of the food in terms of calorific reward.

The waggle dance also conveys direction: a dancing bee indicates this by the angle of the straight run from the vertical. This corresponds to the angle between the sun as seen from the hive entrance and the direction of the food source. Thus, if the food source is 45° to the left of a vertical line drawn from the sun to the ground, then the bee performs the straight section of the waggle dance at an angle of 45° to the left of vertical; if the food source is 45° to the right of a vertical line drawn from the sun to the ground, then she performs her straight run at 45° to the right of vertical.

She is able to impart accurate directional information because she has memorized the position of the sun on her return journey. Her sense of time enables her to compensate for the sun's ever-changing position. Thus, a bee which dances for 30 minutes changes the angle of her straight dance to the vertical by 7–8° of arc.

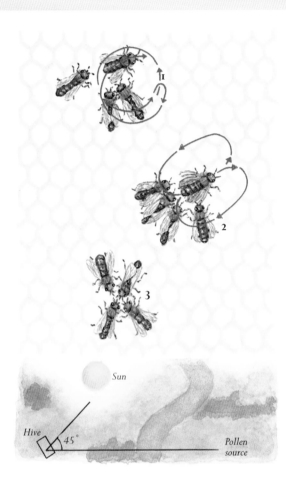

Sun

Hive 45°

Pollen source

For distances between 25 and 100m (80–330ft), workers perform a dance somewhat intermediate between the round dance and the waggle dance.

The information transmitted via the round and waggle dances may be augmented by floral fragrances detected by followers on the dancers' bodies and in samples of nectar they regurgitate (3).

Another type of dance has been observed. This is called the vibrational dance: workers vibrate their bodies rapidly, especially their abdomens, in an up-and-down direction. This dance directs workers to areas of the comb where waggle dances are being performed. Vibrational dances are most frequent at times when the colony's foraging effort needs to be maximized and more workers recruited.

Von Frisch found that the western honeybee has regional dialects. For example, Italian honeybees change from the round dance to the waggle dance when the food source is about 35m (115ft) from the colony, while Austrian bees make this change at 80m (260ft). When Von Frisch mixed the two types of bee in a single hive, the bees with different dialects had the greatest of difficulty in understanding each other; confusion reigned when the food source was between 35 and 80m away.

On occasion, the dance language is used to transmit information other than the source, direction and quality of food. Periodically, honeybee colonies swarm. Part of the colony remains in the hive with a new queen, and the old queen departs with the swarm (see Chapter 7). The swarm clusters on a branch or rock and scout workers seek a new nest site, usually a cavity in a hollow tree or a rock cleft. Returning scouts dance on the surface of the swarm, using the dance language to give information on the distance and direction of a suitable new nest site. In this way, the swarm as a whole, numbering perhaps 50 000 bees, eventually takes up residence at the new nest site.

The dance language of the honeybee is remarkably complex behaviour. It involves a forager remembering visual, directional and calorific data and being able to pass it on to her nest-mates using a system of stereotyped, coded signals, each of which has meaning; together, these signals impart a real message, pregnant with information. For this to work, a nest-mate must be able to perceive, understand and translate this information into a rewarding foraging trip for herself. When she returns, she may well become a dancer in her own right. And all of this complex information transfer takes place in the darkness of the hive.

The processing power of the honeybee brain is impressive. The dance language is a scaled-down re-enactment or mini-charade of the recent foraging trip; it involves transmission of remembered information via posture, gesture, vibration, sound and scent.

Our language conveys information via sounds and written marks which have agreed, symbolic meanings. The dance language of honeybees is a multi-channel system of communication, and also uses coded signals with meaning. It is, therefore, a true language, in the same sense as our own.

array of cues, she may well be memorizing the route *back* to the shrubs, if these prove to be a rich hunting ground and worth further trips.

Learning by experience is the hallmark of ants, wasps and bees. *Polistes* wasps are a good example. There are many species of *Polistes* worldwide. They are social and live in small colonies, making exposed nests of paper out of chewed pieces of wood fibre.

A scientist in America made a study of how *Polistes* wasps handled their caterpillar prey. Every day, he placed caterpillars on the same plant so that he could watch how the wasps dealt with them. The wasps soon learned to associate the arrival of the scientist with the arrival of food. They would fly immediately to the plant and wait to be fed, in just the same way a dog or cat waits by its bowl when it sees its owner pick up a can of food.

ARE INSECTS INTELLIGENT?

Insects can be seen as miniature super-computers. Most of what an insect needs to do to survive long enough to produce offspring is hard-wired into the system – preprogrammed efficiency. But some aspects of an insect's world are just not predictable enough for a strictly prepro-grammed response: the insect computer has to be able to learn and modify its responses. Hence, our smart *Polistes* wasps and the dance language of the honeybee (pages 58–9).

If intelligence is defined in terms of the ability to solve problems, then insects are not intelligent. They do *seem* to be able to solve practical problems, but the reality behind this apparent intelligence is this: the preprogrammed or hard-wired behaviour patterns encoded in its ner-vous system are arranged in such a way that a particular piece of behav-iour is triggered by a combination of both internal physiological rhythms and cycles and sensory input from the outside world.

Advanced insects such as ants, wasps and bees have a vast range of such behaviours and therefore can react to a wide range of both internal and external stimuli. It is this ability which enables them to sustain all the behavioural interactions that make up a complex society.

This is a tribute to the processing abilities of the insect brain and sense organs. But insects are very selective in the information they take on board. Unlike us, they do not overload themselves with irrelevant information. An insect, then, is just as intelligent as it needs to be.

OPPOSITE: *A colony of the social wasp,* Mischocyttarus alfkenii *(Trinidad), attend their nest on the underside of a leaf. Nesting wasps, ants and bees require a high degree of spatial awareness and memory in order to navigate back to their nests.*

3

ON THE MOVE

The running, jumping, flying, swimming and standing still show

Taking to the air, this male harlequin beetle,
Acrocinus longimanus *(Venezuela),*
gets extra lift from its wing cases or elytra.

INSECTS ARE EVERYWHERE. This is because they are very good at getting about. Indeed, their efficiency in travelling has enabled them to invade the remotest of oceanic islands.

Nearly all adult insects have six legs and can walk or crawl. The majority have wings and can fly. Many are adept at jumping and some, such as locusts, can walk, run, jump *and* fly.

LEGS

A male darkling beetle, Onymacris ruhatipennis, amorously chases a potential mate in the Namibian desert. Both beetles are pursued by a lizard, Muroles cuneirostris, so long, running legs are handy for at least two reasons. These beetles are among the fastest things on six legs, covering 1m per second.

Insects have many ways of walking, running and jumping. This is a reflection of the many different places in which they live. Thus, small beetles which live in crevices in bark or under bark would find long legs a distinct disadvantage. Instead, they have short, stubby legs with coarse spines which help them to gain purchase on rough bark or wood. In the normal course of events, such beetles are not often called upon to run. But they can run when, say, they are traversing a piece of dead wood, from one patch of bark to another: being able to run shortens the time they are exposed to the danger of predation.

By contrast, tiger beetles, which chase insect prey over bare ground, have long legs, adapted for running, and are among the fastest runners on earth. Species of *Mantichora*, for example, are capable of relative speeds far greater than a cheetah's, covering 1m per second in pursuit of insect prey in the deserts of southern Africa. Many species of tiger beetle increase their ground-covering capacity by flight-assisted runs, taking to the air momentarily.

Some darkling beetles are just as fast as the tiger beetles. Species of *Onymacris*, found in the extreme deserts of Namibia, use their running abilities not only for chasing mates and avoiding lizards but also in running from one shaded spot to another: being small creatures, desert insects are prone to desiccation and expose themselves to direct sunlight as little as possible. Having long legs like *Onymacris* is not only an adaptation for running fast; they also keep the insect raised, minimizing contact with the burning sand.

Many insects have evolved the ability to jump, either to avoid predators or, in the case of fleas, to gain access to a new bird or mammalian host. Nearly always, the ability to jump involves modified hindlegs, with

OVERLEAF: *Not all legs are used for getting about. The front legs of all praying mantids, like this* Parasphendale agrionina *(Kenya), are adapted for seizing prey.*

BELOW: *Caterpillars of butterflies and moths have short, fleshy pro-legs, as in this emperor moth caterpillar,* Antheraea eucalypti *(Australia).*

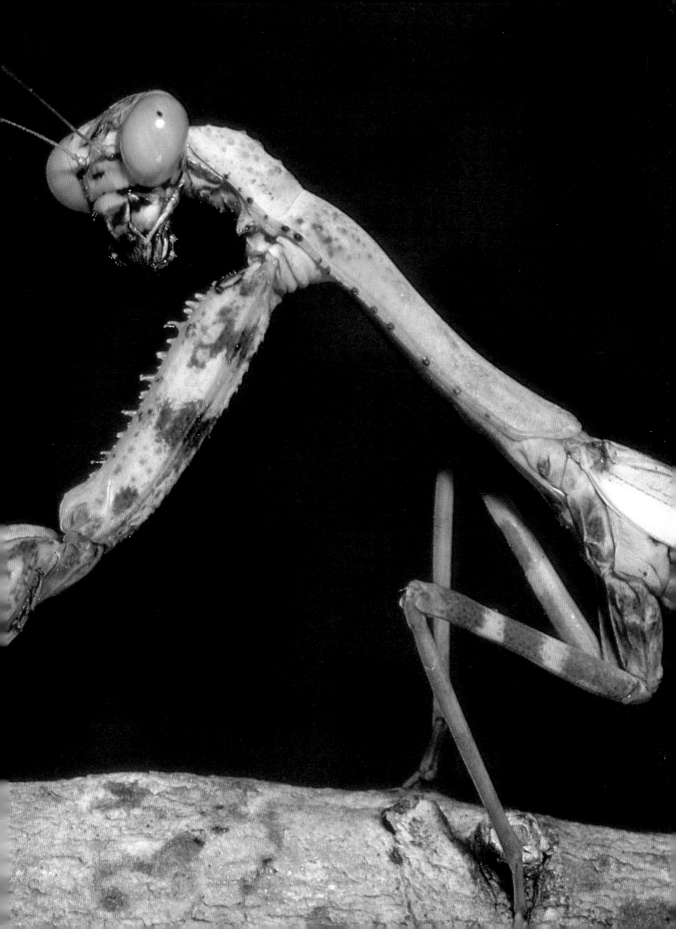

SIX-LEGGED TRIPODS

Six-legged tripods? No, this is not a contradiction in terms. Although the walking insect has six legs, at any one stage only three legs are in contact with the ground. These are always the front and hindlegs of one side and the midleg of the opposite side (see diagram right). The legs not in contact with the ground are brought forward and then make contact with the ground as the three legs formerly in contact are now lifted up and forwards. In this way, the insect takes successive steps, the power strokes being transmitted through the legs in contact with the surface the insect is walking on.

Motion is powered via muscles in the thorax, acting on the bases of the legs, with extension or flexion of the legs transmitted through internal leg muscles (see diagram below). Insects gain purchase on, and leverage against, the surface via paired claws and adhesive pads at the tips of the tarsi.

The mechanics of walking are not under the direct control of the brain; each of the three pairs of legs is controlled by nerve ganglia in the appropriate segment of the thorax. Although there is feedback to the central processor of

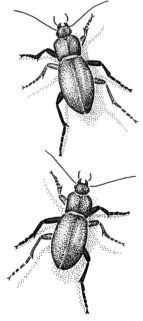

A walking ground beetle, Carabus *sp. The legs depicted in the darker colour are those in contact with the ground.*

the brain, the thoracic ganglia are largely independent: a cleanly decapitated insect will carry on walking, albeit a little unsteadily.

Robot-designers have become interested in the tripod-based gait of walking insects: combined with a low centre of gravity, this gait gives insects enormous stability. In the past, researchers based their designs on the bipedal gait of humans, with all the associated problems of trying to maintain balance. With the stability of designs based on the insect gait, engineers can now concentrate on control and sensory systems. Taking a leaf out of the insects' book, some have sited the control processors for the legs of their robots in the robot's equivalent of the thorax, leaving additional space in the on-board computer or 'brain' for sensory systems such as video cameras and image analysers.

Detailed studies of insect movement and control systems have therefore been an inspiration to robotics engineers. Factories in the future may be operated by robots based on systems which began evolving more than 300 million years ago.

RIGHT: *A unnamed desert darkling beetle leaves a trail of footprints in the Sam sand dunes of Rajasthan (India).*

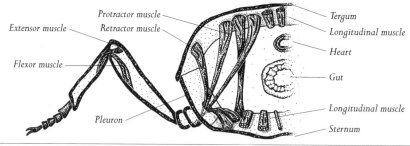

LEFT: *A section through the thorax and legs of an insect, showing the thoracic and leg muscles which operate movement of the legs.*

massive development of the femur, which is packed with muscle.

The prodigious leaps of insects such as grasshoppers and fleas cannot, however, be powered directly by muscles: the nerve impulses are too slow and muscle has a low response rate. Instead, the muscles are used to gradually build up and maintain mechanical tension. In grasshoppers, the tension is stored by the distortion of the tibia of the hindleg. The sudden release of this tension propels the grasshopper into the air.

In fleas, the mechanism is a little more bizarre: they have been called insects which fly with their legs. This is because these wingless parasites use the remnants of the flying apparatus of their winged ancestors in setting themselves up for a leap.

The powerful hind legs of this diving beetle, Dytiscus marginalis *(UK), have their surface area increased with dense fringes of stiff bristles.*

The part in question is called the pleural arch, a modified relict of the wing hinge. This is made of a special protein, resilin, a kind of natural rubber. When a flea gears itself for a jump, muscles at the base of the leg contract and distort the cuticle of the thorax; the rear leg is now raised and the flea is poised to jump. At the same time, what were the flight muscles in the flea's ancestors compress the pleural arch. As this compression is relieved, a burst of stored energy is released and transmitted to the base of the hindleg by a connecting cuticular ridge and the flea leaps into the air, faster than the eye can see and with an audible click.

Resilin is a highly efficient elastic, releasing up to 97 per cent of its stored energy, and this propels the flea with a G-force of up to 140. The cat flea, *Ctenocephalides felis*, can easily jump 34cm (over 13in), the equivalent of a 1.83m (6ft) tall human athlete being able to perform a high jump of 31m (102ft). And a hungry flea, in search of a host, can jump 600 times per hour for up to three days.

Many insects are aquatic and use modified legs as oars. Water bugs, *Corixa* spp., and diving beetles, *Dytiscus* spp., for example, have dense fringes of articulating hairs in their legs. On the power stroke, the hairs splay out, increasing the surface area of the leg and hence the resistance exerted by it against the water; on the return stroke, the hairs bend at the base, lie flat along the leg and reduce the resistance to the water.

A WORKSHOP OF LEGS

LEFT: *Short, fleshy pro-legs armed with claws enable this moth caterpillar,* Apopestes spectrum *(Israel), to both walk and grip the edge of the leaf on which it feeds.*

BELOW: *A mating pair of flower beetles,* Genyodonta flavomaculata *(South Africa). The claws of the male's elongate forelegs are adapted for holding on to the female.*

Insects have evolved a bewildering variety of legs, each adapted for a special purpose. Apart from the obvious specializations for high speed running, or jumping, adaptations range from the raptorial (prey grasping) legs of praying mantids and some assassin bugs, to the short, flattened and multi-spined digging legs of mole crickets, dung beetles and some ground beetles.

Male diving beetles have large suction pads on the undersides of their forelegs for holding on to the female during mating. Some male bees have dense fringes of thick, stiff hairs on the forelegs which cover the eyes of the female during mating: they act as blinkers to screen visual cues from rival males. And, as we shall see in Chapter 4, female bees have a variety of modified leg structures for the transport of pollen.

The list of leg modifications is seemingly endless and testifies to the amazing evolutionary capabilities of insects: if there is a specialized job involving legs, somewhere there is an insect making a living at it.

RIGHT: *Massively developed, muscle-packed hindlegs make this South African savannah grasshopper nymph,* Zonocerus elegans, *a powerful leaper.*

BELOW: *This mole cricket from Trinidad,* Gryllotalpa spp., *has forelegs highly modified for digging underground tunnels, where it feeds at the roots of plants.*

RIGHT: *The viciously spined forelegs of this unnamed praying mantis from Costa Rica are beautifully adapted for grasping and holding insect prey.*

STANDING STILL

For some insects, staying put is the name of the game. Female vapourer moths, for example, have no functional wings. As soon as a female emerges from her silk cocoon, she attracts a mate by emitting a scent. Then she lays her eggs on the remains of the cocoon and dies.

Parasitic insects, such as lice, having found a host, have a vested interest in staying put. They have modified, prehensile claws with which to hang on to the feathers or hairs of their host.

The species of lice adapted to live on people differ in the structure of their claws, which reflects their different habitats. Thus, the human head louse, *Pediculus capitis*, and the human body louse, *P. humanus*, both have relatively narrow, long prehensile claws, adapted to hang on to the finer hairs of the head and body, which are mostly circular in section. The pubic louse (crab louse), *Pthirus pubis*, by contrast, has shorter, wider prehensile claws, adapted to grasp the coarser hairs of the pubic region, which are flat in section.

In the forests of South America, there are five species of moth which also have a vested interest in staying put for most of the time. These are females of sloth moths, so called because the adults spend much of their time roosting in the coarse body hairs of sloths.

The best known of these moths is *Cryptoses choloepi*. It can fly much faster than the 1mph which is the best that their slow-moving hosts can achieve. But they remain on board until a relatively rare event occurs: defecation by the sloth. It takes up to three months for food to pass through the sloth's gut, and it urinates and defecates only once a week.

When the sloth defecates, the moths leave its fur and lay their eggs in the sloth's droppings. The caterpillars feed and pupate in the droppings and the new generation of adults then flies off in search of sloths on which to hitch a ride.

WINGS

The evolution of wings set the seal on the insect success story: flight has enabled them to be the ultimate explorers, colonizers of the entire globe. With their flexible design and their potential for rapid evolution, insects have invaded all parts of the world, including some of the most extreme environments on the planet.

A male carpenter bee, Xylocopa spp. (Kenya), hovers in his mating territory. Hovering and its ultra-high frequency of wingbeats not only requires finely tuned neuromuscular control, it also requires ready access to high energy food, in this case nectar.

The fossil record shows that there have been winged insects for at least 305 million years. There are no fossils of insects which are intermediate between the wingless and winged state, so we can only speculate about how wings evolved and what structures became modified to form them.

It has been postulated that wings originated among aquatic insects as paddle-like outgrowths from the sides of the thorax and were involved in swimming. A more recent suggestion is based on observations of modern mayflies and stoneflies, ancient groups of insects more than 250 million years old. Both groups have aquatic larvae and flying adults. The adults are often seen skimming along the surface film of calm water, using their wings as paddles. The suggestion is that wings originated as paddles to enable adult insects to skim the surface film of water.

Even short, stubby wings would be effective because the insect's body weight is supported by the water, so the usual considerations of power-to-weight ratios would not apply. And the longer the wings, the faster the insects could skim. If there was strong natural selection for longer, more powerful wings for skimming, then wings may have evolved beyond the critical power-to-weight ratio for flight, and the potential to fly was arrived at almost by accident.

FLIGHT: THE POWER SYSTEMS

Flying insects have two pairs of wings. The wings of insects are membranous extensions from the side of the thorax. The membrane is supported by veins, which are thickenings of the cuticle forming the wing. Cross-veins join the major veins and increase rigidity. The veins contain tracheae, nerve fibres and blood vessels.

The wings are powered by muscles in the thorax, but in two very different ways. In the more primitive insects, such as cockroaches and dragonflies, the wings are powered by direct muscles. This means that the muscles are attached directly to the wing bases. There are two sets, one for the upstroke, one for the downstroke (see diagram right).

Although the direct muscle flight system is an old and primitive design, dragonflies are superb aerial acrobats and are highly manoeuvrable: in a tight turn, a dragonfly can exert a force of 2.5G.

In the more advanced insects, the wings are powered by two sets of indirect muscles. Instead of being attached to the wing bases, one set is attached to the upper wall (tergum) and lower wall (sternum), and the other set is attached to the front and back of the thorax.

Contraction of the muscles attached to the tergum causes the tergum to be pulled down and, with it, the base of the wing; this forces the wing into an upstroke. Contraction of the muscles which run from the front to the back of the thorax deforms the thoracic box and the wings are thrown into a downstroke. A split-second relaxation of one set of muscles at the end of either an upstroke or a downstroke allows the elasticity of the thoracic box to regain its shape and be poised for the next muscle contraction.

This 'click' mechanism can be likened to a small tin box with a convex lid: press the lid between thumb and forefinger and the lid and bottom of the tin both bow inwards; release the pressure, and the tin regains its shape with an audible click.

Indirect flight muscles are found in the butterflies and moths, beetles, flies, ants, wasps and bees. Such insects do have direct wing muscles, but they are not involved in power production; instead, they are concerned with the orientation of the wings, the angles the wings take up relative to the direction of flight in order to compensate for cross winds or tight turns.

Some insect groups increase their aerodynamic

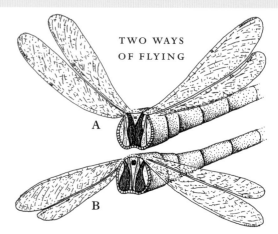

TWO WAYS OF FLYING

ABOVE: *A section through a dragonfly thorax, illustrating direct flight muscles (those in action are shown in colour).* **A** *shows those effecting the up-stroke of wings,* **B** *those effecting the down-stroke. A section through a fly thorax (*RIGHT*), depicts indirect flight muscles.* **C** *shows those effecting the up-stroke,* **D** *those effecting the down-stroke.*

efficiency by coupling the forewings and hindwings together; this makes for better control. Some butterflies and moths do this with one or more bristles on the leading edge of the hindwings, which latch into a retaining structure on the hind edge of the forewings. Some caddisflies and all ants, wasps and bees have a row of hooks on the leading edge of the hindwing and these engage a fold on the trailing edge of the forewing.

The greatest aerodynamic efficiency is found in the true, two-winged flies, such as the bluebottle, houseflies, horseflies and robberflies. The hindwings have been converted into a pair of remarkable balancing organs, the halteres. Each is club-shaped, with a well-developed terminal knob.

When in flight, the halteres beat in time with the wings, but out of phase. The knob is heavier than the rest of the haltere and this keeps it beating in one direction. If the fly makes a sudden change in direction, either voluntarily or because of a gust of wind, the stem of the haltere is twisted; a dense array of sensors in the

ABOVE: *This resting male hallowe'en pennant dragonfly,* Celithemis eponina *(Florida, USA), shows the dense pattern of veins which add support and rigidity to the wing membranes.*

BELOW: *In flies, it is the hindwings which have become highly modified. They form a pair of drumstick-shaped structures called halteres, seen here in a cranefly,* Tipula paludosa *(UK).*

stem feeds postural data to the brain and the fly can adjust its flying attitude and maintain straight and level flight. With its two on-board stabilizing gyroscopes, the fly is like a tiny fly-by-wire aircraft.

Insects with indirect flight muscles are able to generate an enormous power output: even slow butterflies have a wingbeat frequency of 5 per second, while bees operate at about 180 per second. But the record is held jointly by tiny midges and some hoverflies, which are capable of wingbeat frequencies greater than 1000 per second.

Hoverflies' wings beat at this phenomenal rate when they are living up to their name – hovering, their wings getting nowhere fast. In their rapid darting flight, they achieve speeds of 16kph (10mph).

The fastest insects are found among tropical wasps and bees, which may attain speeds of up to 72kph (45mph). Weight for weight, insects produce about the same power output as an aircraft piston engine, or about 30 times the power of human leg muscles.

OPPOSITE: *The wing membranes of flying insects are supported by a network of thickened veins, as in this roosting lantern-fly (not a fly, but a bug),* Pyrops sp. *(Malaysia).*

BELOW: *The forewings of beetles have become modified into horny cases or elytra, to protect the membranous hindwings when not in flight. However, the stiff elytra are not lost to the cause of flight: they provide lift, as, here, a South African longhorn beetle,* Tragocephala variegata, *takes to the air.*

Unlike pterodactyls, birds and bats, insects have not had to lose any limbs in order to fly; the wings of all other flying creatures have evolved from their forelegs. Insects, then, have all six legs free when on the ground. Beetles have an additional adaptation for an active life on the ground or among vegetation: they use only their hindwings for flight, their forewings having become tough, horny wing cases. These protect the delicate, membranous wings when the beetle is on the ground. Most beetles can fly readily when necessary but, when on the ground, they can run through crevices in soil and bark and through leaf litter, with their hindwings safely stowed away. Wing cases are probably the secret of the beetles' success. And successful they truly are, if numbers of species are anything to go by: they represent 32 per cent of all animal species. If flies are masters of the air, then beetles are masters of the ground below.

Whatever the details of the evolution of flight, the aerial abilities of insects have been of great survival value. They enable the adults of species with leaf-eating larvae to find new host plants on which to lay eggs. And flight is an integral part of finding a mate for most insects.

LEFT: *A hummingbird hawkmoth,* Macroglossum stellatum *(UK), hovers while refuelling with nectar from flowers of garden stock.*

RIGHT: *A male of the bizarre giraffe-necked leaf-rolling weevil,* Trachelophorus giraffa *(Madagascar), takes to the air, having used a leaf as a vantage point.*

ABOVE: *A helicon butterfly,* Heliconius erato favorinus *(Peru). This species and its relatives have a delicate, fluttering flight, suggested by the narrow, rounded wings and the slim thorax which contains the flight muscles.*

RIGHT: *By contrast, this skipper butterfly,* Jemaida *spp. (Columbia), has a rapid, darting flight, reflected in the broad, blunt wings and the massively developed thorax housing the powerful flight muscles.*

DISPERSAL AND MIGRATION

Many insects which live in narrowly proscribed habitats make short-range dispersal flights. Most ants and termites that we see are wingless, but their sexual forms have wings and, after mating, the females fly in search of a suitable place in which to found a new colony. Adult water bugs and diving beetles may fly from one pond to another if the original pond begins to dry out. For insects such as wood-boring beetles or dung beetles, their specialist habitats are not evenly distributed. Thus a dung beetle, seeking a new dung pat, may have to cross an ocean of grass to find a new one. Having wings facilitates this migration on a small scale.

Being able to fly enables many insects to migrate on a larger scale, away from seasonal extremes of climate, and the consequences may be spectacular. Every year, thousands of bogong moths, *Agrotis infusa*, assemble in the crevices of a few granite outcrops near Canberra, Australia. They migrate over long distances to avoid the heat of the lowlands, and the aggregations are so dense that the wings of the serried ranks of moths look like the overlapping tiles of a roof.

This kind of mass migration is widespread, and it is typical for huge, widely dispersed populations to migrate to a few roosting sites at the same time each year. There is a deep valley in Rhodes, the so-called (and

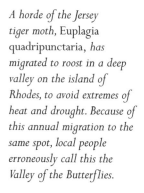

A horde of the Jersey tiger moth, Euplagia quadripunctaria, *has migrated to roost in a deep valley on the island of Rhodes, to avoid extremes of heat and drought. Because of this annual migration to the same spot, local people erroneously call this the Valley of the Butterflies.*

misnamed!) Valley of the Butterflies, where each summer millions of the Jersey tiger moth, *Euplagia quadripunctaria*, congregate in very dull weather. And in California, a species of ladybird (ladybug), *Hippodamia convergens*, migrates in late spring each year from the hot, dry Central Valley to the cool of the Sierra Nevada mountains. In so doing, the ladybirds exploit their flying capabilities to the full: they fly up until they are about one mile high. They are then carried by the seasonally prevailing winds to the mountains. Here, they assemble in their millions on tree trunks. They spend the winter here and make the return journey to the Central Valley early in the following spring. Again, they use the same tactics, but this time the prevailing winds are conveniently in the opposite direction.

Local food shortages and unseasonal changes in the weather stimulate migration in moths and butterflies. Thus, the diamond-backed moth, *Plutella xylostella*, which is only 15mm long, regularly crosses the North Sea to reach Britain and often flies across the Mediterranean. The painted lady butterfly, *Vanessa cardui*, regularly makes mass movements across Europe and has now spread so far that it is found in nearly all parts of the world.

The greatest insect migrant is the monarch butterfly, *Danaus plexippus*. Apart from its regular migrations across the North American continent (see pages 82–3), it has managed to find its way to such distant parts as Australia, New Zealand and Hawaii, where it is now established. After strong, persistent westerly winds, this butterfly occasionally ends up in Britain but, in the absence of the correct food plant for its caterpillars, it cannot survive there.

Relatively few insects are strong enough flyers to make active flight across ocean barriers, but many are borne passively on the wind: they get caught in up-welling thermals, get carried out over the sea by regional air flows and may eventually be lucky enough to make landfall in some hospitable place. Thus, while active migration is responsible for only a tiny proportion of the insect faunas of distant islands, passive and chance dispersal, given enough time, is sufficient to populate all islands. But this literally would not have got off the ground in the first place without the insects' ability to fly. This colonization of new islands is one of the most dramatic consequences of insect flight.

That there is a constant rain of windborne insects is indicated by the lava crickets of Hawaii, *Caconemobius* spp. These crickets, the first in the

MIGRATING MONARCHS

The annual migrations across America of the monarch butterfly, *Danaus plexippus*, are one of the wonders of the insect world. In autumn, tens of millions fly south and roost in vast numbers on trees in selected sites. The butterflies use the same trees year after year.

About 5 million monarchs from south-west Canada and the north-western USA migrate to coastal California, where they overwinter at 45 roosting sites; at least 100 million from the eastern half of southern Canada and the eastern half of the USA migrate to Mexico, where they roost at only 11 sites in volcanic mountains of central Mexico (see map opposite). They cluster in such vast numbers that sometimes the weight of butterflies is sufficient to break off branches.

In spring, the populations which overwinter in California make for the Central Valley and the base of the western slopes of the Sierra Nevada. Here they die after laying eggs on milkweeds, *Asclepias* spp., the special foodplant of the caterpillars. Those which overwinter in Mexico fly to the Gulf region of the

United States, where they in their turn die after laying their eggs.

The next generation of butterflies moves further inland; they lay their eggs and, in this way, up to five generations leapfrog each other until the northern limits of the monarch's range has been recolonized.

Individual butterflies of the generations which move north in the spring and early summer fly only a few hundred miles; those of the last autumn generation, which make the southern journey, cover distances of up to 4800km (2980 miles). Entomologists have tagged individual butterflies and found that it takes them only a few days to cover 1900km (1180 miles), with average speeds of up to 130km (80 miles) per day. Migrants on their way south fly at altitudes up to 1000m (3280ft), riding the winds and expending relatively little energy; they regularly feed at flowers for nectar to maintain their deposits of fat, which represent fuel reserves.

Just how the monarchs navigate is uncertain. It has been suggested that they may use sun-compass

ABOVE: *Recognizing the tourist potential of overwintering aggregations of monarch butterflies, Mexican authorities have erected this sign asking motorists to slow down for migrating monarchs.*

LEFT: *A dense overwintering aggregation of monarch butterflies roosts on a tree in El Rosario, Mexico.*

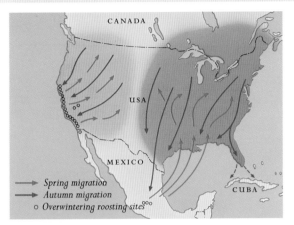

ABOVE: *The migrating monarch: the summer range of the western population is shown in the light colour, the range of the eastern in the darker colour.*

BELOW: *A migrating monarch butterfly,* Danaus plexippus *(USA), refuels on nectar at a flower.*

navigation, or a sense of the earth's magnetic field.

Monarch butterflies migrate for two reasons. First, they travel south because neither the eggs, larvae, pupae nor adults can withstand the freezing winter weather of northern and central continental climates. Secondly, the larval foodplants do not grow in the overwintering sites in California and Mexico, so the spring generations which fly north are migrating to regions where the plants are plentiful.

The correct larval foodplants are vital. The caterpillars sequester poisons from the leaves, which they use for chemical defence (see Chapter 5).

Unfortunately, the migration of monarchs is now under some threat. Urban development in California and logging activities in Mexico have reduced the number of roosting sites. There is some hope that growing eco-tourism is making the protection of these sites an economically attractive proposition, but this needs to be managed in a more monarch-friendly way than hitherto.

A carnivorous caterpillar of a Hawaiian moth, Eupithecia orichloris, *eats a lacewing it has caught. These wait-and-pounce, surprise-attack predators occupy the niche usually taken by praying mantids, but these are absent from Hawaii.*

succession of insects to colonize newly cooled lava flows, feed entirely on windborne insects which died in the process and landed on the lava.

We have other evidence that passive dispersal by wind is efficient from the well-developed insect faunas of oceanic islands; by definition, these islands arose from the sea floor and never had any direct connection with any continents.

A startling example of dispersal is found among species of *Timulla*, mutillid wasps whose larvae develop as parasites of the full-grown larvae and pupae of wasps and bees. At first sight, the females of mutillid wasps would seem to be poor candidates for dispersal to islands, oceanic or otherwise, and for one simple reason: they are wingless. The males, however, are fully winged and capable of flight. Indeed, as part of their mating ritual, male mutillids carry their mates in flight, using specially modified mandibles and genitalia.

In 1883 the island of Krakatoa, between Sumatra and Java, suffered a massive volcanic explosion, which completely destroyed the flora and fauna. It is about 25km (15.5 miles) from the nearest land. Within a few years, male and female mutillid wasps were among many insects found on the island. This proves that passive dispersal can be effective in getting insects to newly formed or oceanic islands, even mutillids where one sex is wingless.

When insects arrive at an oceanic island, they may find habitats and climates which are very different from their natural ones. If these are within ranges that the new arrivals can tolerate, and suitable food is there, then the insects will survive. But they may find that things are radically different in other respects: an oceanic island will not have the full spectrum of animals and plants as the insects' area of origin. Some important groups may be absent, including predators. This creates opportunities for the immigrants in the form of unoccupied ecological niches. Indeed, so many new opportunities may present themselves that colonizers eventually undergo explosive evolution, evolving many new species to exploit the available, unoccupied niches. And many insects, having successfully arrived at an island, lose their ability to fly: it is as though one great adventure in their evolutionary past was enough.

Many examples of insects invading new niches are provided by the islands of Hawaii. Here, there are caterpillars of several moth species which think they are praying mantids. Mantids are not native to Hawaii, so the niche for surprise-attack predatory insects was vacant. The vacancy was filled by the caterpillars of several species of *Eupithecia*, which resemble twigs and sit motionless. When an insect inadvertently walks over one and contacts special hairs, this triggers a lightning response: the caterpillar lashes out with specially modified front legs, seizes the prey and eats it.

Hawaii provides yet more good examples. The islands are very young by geological standards, having been formed a mere 800 000 years ago. There are 500 species of fruitflies unique to the archipelago, all descended from a few chance colonizers. Indeed, there are 6500 species of insects which are unique to Hawaii, and it is thought that they are descended from just 250 species which managed to cross the Pacific by chance dispersal.

The ability to fly has been a major factor in the insect success story. And insect flight has had a profound ecological impact on the planet as a whole: the vast majority of flowering plants, including our crops, exploit flying insects as unwitting agents of pollination. Flying insects, either as help-mates in the sex lives of plants, or as colonizers of oceanic islands, contribute to the creation and maintenance of biodiversity.

4

ULTIMATE CONSUMERS

Food and feeding

*Caterpillars of an unnamed emperor moth
feed communally on a leaf (Brazil).*

A MAJOR THEME IN the lives of insects is diversity through special-ization. This is reflected in the enormous range of diets found among them. And this is possible because of their amazing flex-ibility of design: the vast numbers of insect species are extraordinarily efficient at dividing up resources between themselves.

Insects include among their numbers herbivores, carnivores and scavengers; omnivores are relatively rare. Many species are specialists not only in what they eat, but how they set about finding or trapping their food. And many have evolved close, symbiotic relationships with each other, with plants or with micro-organisms.

TOOLS FOR THE JOB

Insects have mouthparts designed either for biting and chewing or piercing and sucking (see pages 90–91). The biters and chewers include the dragonflies and damselflies, cockroaches, grasshoppers, locusts, crickets, mantids, stick insects, earwigs and beetles. Moths and butter-flies have biting mouthparts in their caterpillar stages and sucking mouthparts as adults.

One primitive group of moths retains functional jaws and specializes in chewing pollen grains. The caterpillars of these moths occupy a dif-ferent niche: they graze on mosses.

Insects which feed on enclosed fluids such as sap or blood have mouthparts adapted for piercing *and* sucking, and include lice, bugs, thrips, fleas and some flies such as robberflies, midges and mosquitoes.

Liquid food which is readily accessible, such as nectar, urine and the fluids of faeces and putrescent corpses, is imbibed with sucking mouth-parts by insects such as flies, butterflies and moths.

The wasps, ants and bees seem to break the rules: all species have both biting and sucking mouthparts, though the jaws are not often used in feeding. Instead, they are used in nest construction and the manipula-tion of building materials such as leaves, resin and wax.

Hunting wasps such as *Ammophila* spp. and short-tongued bumble-bees such as *Bombus terrestris* may use their jaws indirectly for feeding by gaining access to food. For example, after catching and stinging her prey – a caterpillar, say – a female *Ammophila* uses her jaws to squeeze out body fluids from the caterpillar, which she then sucks up, before taking her prey back to her nest where she will store it as food for her larvae.

OPPOSITE: *Using its biting mouthparts, this bush cricket (katydid),* Euconocephalus *sp. (Australia), crushes the anthers of a flower to eat pollen.*

A CUTLER'S NIGHTMARE

The diversity of insects and their feeding habits is reflected in the tremendous range of modifications to their mouthparts. Insects which specialize on liquid food have mouthparts whose basic components have fused to form a sucking tube; those which feed on sap or blood are also modified for piercing.

The original biting and chewing structures are retained by those species which eat solid food. Bees and wasps have both sucking and biting mouthparts but, in nearly all species, the jaws are used to manipulate nest-building material rather than feeding.

ABOVE: *This brush-snouted weevil,* Rhina barbirostris *(Costa Rica), has a pair of tiny jaws at the tip of its long snout.*

RIGHT: *A water bug, the so-called water scorpion,* Nepa cineraria *(UK), sucks the blood of a stickleback, having used its tubular mouthparts to inject lethal venom.*

RIGHT: *A female harlequin beetle,* Acrocinus longimanus *(Trinidad), uses her powerful jaws to bite a hole in wood into which she will lay her eggs. She is covered with hundreds of tiny red mites which scavenge on organic matter adhering to her.*

LEFT: *A soldier worker of the leafcutter ant,* Atta bisphaerica *(Brazil), uses its powerful jaws to cut up a fruit. The massively developed head contains powerful muscles to work the jaws, which are used in defence as well as processing food and nest materials.*

Workers of *Bombus terrestris* will bite holes into the base of long-tubed flowers such as comfrey to gain access to the nectaries; their tongues are too short to reach the nectar by the legitimate route.

HERBIVORES

More than half of all insects are plant feeders, and about 5 per cent of all leaves are eventually eaten by insects. Roots, stems and flowers are also attacked. In temperate forests, caterpillars are the main chewers of leaves, and occasionally species such as the gypsy moth, *Lymantria dispar*, undergo population explosions and cause massive defoliation. The caterpillars of *L. dispar* eat the leaves of a wide range of deciduous trees, and are serious pests of orchards.

In warmer climates, beetles are the most prevalent leaf eaters and sometimes cause defoliation. In Australia, for example, the so-called Christmas beetles, *Anoplognathus* spp., sometimes cause extensive damage to eucalyptus trees.

The overall average leaf area lost to insect herbivores in forests is surprisingly constant, at about 8.8 per cent for both temperate and tropical forests. Nevertheless, even in natural vegetation, in non-outbreak conditions, 20–45 per cent of leaves may be consumed. Crop monocultures, though, are particularly susceptible to insects (see Chapter 8) and 100 per cent defoliation is possible in severe pest outbreaks. On an annual basis, an average of 20 per cent of crops is lost to insects.

The loss of leaves to herbivores is potentially dangerous for plants. Leaves are the organs of food manufacture by photosynthesis, the process whereby radiant energy from the sun is captured by the green pigment, chlorophyll, and used to power the synthesis of starch from carbon dioxide and water.

Sap-suckers, such as aphids, pose other threats: apart from debilitating plants through the loss of sap, they also transmit viruses.

Like all plant-feeding bugs, tree hoppers such as these Antianthe expansa *(Mexico) tap into the flowing sap of plants with their piercing and sucking mouthparts.*

Plants, however, are not helpless: after conquering the land and having things their own way for several million years, they had to adapt to a new threat in the form of insects. They began to evolve many ingenious ways of defending themselves and the stage was set for an evolutionary arms race which, after hundreds of millions of years, is still going on.

A simple way a plant can defend itself is to make its leaves mechanically difficult to handle. Many species have spiny or very hairy leaves, or have dense networks of very tough, woody veins. Others, especially the grasses, lay down silica in their leaves, so the grazing caterpillar experiences, in effect, a mouthful of ground glass.

A plant with tough leaves can have profound effects on insects. Research in North America, for example, has shown that the reproductive success of the chrysomelid beetle, *Pladiodera versicolora*, can be undermined by the willow leaves its larvae and adults feed on: old, tough leaves are four times harder than young tender ones.

After one sample of 40 newly emerged beetles was fed on old leaves for a month, their jaws were 13 per cent shorter than those of a similar sample which had been fed on young leaves; beetles with worn-down jaws were slower and less efficient in processing the food and, as a result, the females laid fewer eggs than those fed on young leaves. Another consequence of feeding on tough leaves is that the beetles have to feed for longer periods and so are exposed to greater risks of predation.

Very many plant species use chemical warfare against insects. They manufacture chemicals which are not directly involved in the plant's metabolism. Instead, they are laid down in the tissues, principally leaves, which come under attack.

These chemicals are the so-called secondary plant compounds (SPCs) and include alkaloids, cyanide and sulphur compounds, resins, tannins and essential oils. SPCs work in a number of ways. Some, such as the essential oils, simply deter insects; others, such as alkaloids and the cyanide compounds, are toxic and many compounds inhibit egg-laying. (See also Chapter 5.)

Tannins bind with proteins in the insects' gut, and thus render the leaves indigestible or reduce their nutritive value. SPCs which act in this way are called antinutritive substances.

It is interesting that some of these SPCs are palatable to people and are sought for culinary uses or as the basis of attractive scents. Thus the

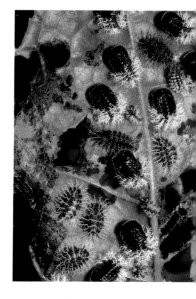

ABOVE: *Both larvae and adults of leaf beetles (Chrysomelidae) use their biting mouthparts to graze on the surface cells of leaves, creating a characteristic skeletonization of the leaves.*

OVERLEAF: *A grasshopper, Chromacris colorata (Mexico), eats a poisonous member of the potato family. The warning colours of the grasshopper signal that it has sequestered the plant's poisons for its own defence.*

RIGHT: *A shieldbug,*
Peromatus *sp. (Brazil),*
sucks sap. Many other
shieldbugs feed on the body
fluids of other insects.

essential oils in herbs such as rosemary, thyme, lavender and garlic, evolved as part of the chemical warfare against insects and disease organisms, have been hijacked by us for our own uses.

SPCs can be expensive for the plant to manufacture: they divert energy that could be devoted to photosynthesis. Some plants have evolved a way of reducing the cost. Instead of making the SPC continuously, they mobilize it only when insect damage occurs.

As we might have predicted, some insects have evolved a neat way of overcoming this defensive ploy. Larvae of the ladybird (ladybug) *Epilachna cucurbitae* literally circumvent the cucumber plant's delivery system of chemical weapons: they select an area of leaf on which to feed and bite through the veins which supply it before the chemicals can be mobilized. They then feed on the leaf patch they have so effectively disarmed.

This is a world of evolutionary arms races, of measures, counter-measures and escalation. Just as we have hijacked some SPCs for our own purposes, so many insects have turned the tables on plants: they have evolved ways of disarming the plant by detoxifying plant poisons and many have become chemical hijackers in their own right: they sequester the plants' chemical weapons and use them for their own defensive strategies against insectivorous reptiles and birds (see Chapter 5). Some species have been so successful in turning the tables on plants that the SPCs actually stimulate feeding behaviour in the insects.

OPPOSITE: *Caterpillars have*
biting mouthparts and
usually bite into the edge of
the leaf, as with this
frangipani hawkmoth larva,
Pseudosphinx tetrio
(Brazil). The bright livery is
a warning to would-be
predators that this larva is
distasteful.

With some plants, the escalation has gone further and started a chain of bizarre evolutionary knock-on effects. In North America, some types of clover, *Trifolium* spp., have adopted indirect rather than direct chemical warfare against caterpillars of the moth *Plathypena scabra*. (The caterpillars are known as green cloverworms.) Somehow, the plants detect when some leaves have been damaged and release chemicals which do not affect the feeding caterpillar. Rather, they attract an enemy of the caterpillar, calling for reinforcements in the form of female parasitic wasps, which lay their eggs inside the body of the caterpillar.

The story does not end here, though. The cloverworm has evolved a way out: when it detects a parasitic wasp, it launches itself off the edge of the leaf, attached by a silken lifeline. This is sufficient to put off most species of parasitic wasp. But there is one species, *Protomicroplitis facetosa*, which is not deterred, having evolved a neat little response: it abseils down the silk thread, stings the caterpillar to paralyse it temporarily and lays its eggs inside it. The caterpillar recovers and climbs up the thread, but is doomed: the growing wasp larvae gradually kill it as they eat its insides. There is an additional twist to the story: the caterpillar continues to feed, and the fact that it *is* parasitized attracts another species of parasitic wasp, *Mesochorus discitergus*.

Once again, the caterpillar throws itself off the leaf, attached to its lifeline of silk. But this second wasp can deal with that. Instead of abseiling down the thread to the caterpillar, it hauls it up to the leaf. Here, it stings the caterpillar and lays its eggs in it. The sting in the tale is that the larvae of this wasp are parasites of the larvae of the first wasp.

The caterpillar-like larvae of the primitive wasps called sawflies have biting mouthparts and eat leaves. Almost all species are dietary specialists, such as these larvae of Croesus septentrionalis *(UK), which feed on alder.*

An acorn weevil, Balaninus glandium *(UK), withdraws its snout from an acorn. Despite appearances, the weevil does not have sucking mouthparts; like all beetles, it has a pair of jaws, in this case mounted at the tip of the long snout or rostrum.*

This charming vignette of life in North American clover fields illustrates the impact insects have on ecosystems. A single adaptation on the part of one species sets off a chain of evolutionary events as insects live up to their reputation as the world's greatest opportunists: initially, pressure from insect herbivores led clovers to evolve chemical defences. Cloverworms evolved a way to deal with this, so the clovers evolved the means to recruit parasitic wasps to their aid. In response to this, the caterpillars developed their Indian rope trick strategy. The parasitic wasps in turn evolved two ways of overcoming this ploy. In this escalating arms race, each player in the game has become an ultra specialist, carving out a piece of the action which is unique to itself.

Herbivorous insects can have far-reaching effects on their host plants: they can influence the plant's growth, architecture and even its sexual expression. In the south-western United States, larvae of the moth *Dioryctria albovitella* bore into the stems and cones of pinyon pines, *Pinus edulis*. In stands of trees of the same age, some are low, and shrubby in form, others are tall, erect and tree-like. These differences in architecture reflect the pattern of feeding by the moth larvae. In the short, shrubby individuals, the moths had destroyed the terminal buds of the shoots. By contrast, the tall, erect trees had lost three to six times

SWARMING LOCUSTS

A swarm of the African desert locust, *Schistocerca gregaria*, is an awesome sight. Covering an area of 1000 square kilometres (400 square miles), it may literally blot out the sun. It may contain as many as 50 thousand million individuals, with a density of 50 million per square kilometre (125 million per square mile). Such a swarm is in search of food, and will feed voraciously on the first patch of green vegetation it comes across.

A man battles though a swarm of the desert locust, Schistocerca gregaria, *in North Africa.*

Locusts, however, do not always live and fly in swarms. Most of the time they live as solitary insects, just another kind of short-horned grasshopper. They are dark and mottled and blend well with the arid background of their desert home in North Africa.

So long as drought is a daily fact of life, the locusts remain solitary creatures. But if rain comes and starts a flush of new, green vegetation, then things change drastically. The locusts feed voraciously, the rates of mating and egg-laying increase and a new generation of nymphs appears. Instead of avoiding each other, as before, the nymphs become gregarious and congregate in large groups. As they go through their development, moulting their cuticle five times, they change drastically in appearance: instead of the drab, mottled creatures of before, they assume a bright, conspicuous livery of yellow, orange and black stripes.

They spend long periods roosting on vegetation. It pays the solitary phase to be drab and well camouflaged: this affords protection against predation by birds. But for the gregarious phase, there is safety in numbers: the risk to the individual becomes slight,

LEFT: *Powerful jaws make a single desert locust a formidable eating machine, while (*RIGHT*) force of numbers can make them an occasional threat to human societies.*

and the bright colours make it easier for the nymphs to assemble.

If the rains continue, the bands of marching hoppers increase in size as groups begin to combine, marching across the desert in search of food. Their numbers now are so large that food is a diminishing resource and they spend more and more time on the march.

After the fifth moult, the new adults take to the wing: a swarm is born as they fly *en masse* in search of a new patch of green vegetation.

The adults of this gregarious phase are so different in appearance from the solitary phase that they were, until quite recently, regarded as two different species.

The changes in phase involve not only appearance and behaviour but also physiology and ecology. And the swarming behaviour is an adaptation for migrating to new areas where there is food.

The swarm is at the mercy of the winds, and follows weather fronts until a suitable feeding area is found. Here, the swarm will eat itself out of house and home and then move on again. Swarms can cause tremendous damage to crops. In 1957, a swarm of the desert locust destroyed 167 000 tons of grain. This is enough to feed a million people for a year: even today, a swarm can leave famine in its wake.

Eventually, the swarm finds a suitable place in which to mate and lay eggs. This may give rise to a new swarm, or, if drought occurs, the new generation will be of the solitary phase.

Occasionally, the winds blow a swarm out to sea and they eventually perish. More than a hundred years ago, a huge swarm in South Africa, which covered an area of 5178 sq km (2000 sq miles) was blown out to sea. Eventually, the tides brought the corpses back to shore and these formed a wall 1.2m (4ft) deep, which extended along the coast for 80km (50 miles).

The desert locust is only one of several species which can swarm, and areas of the Middle East, India, Central and South East Asia, Australia and North and South America can be affected.

In South America, some grasshoppers which have not previously been known to go through a gregarious and swarming phase have started to do so, with some detriment to agriculture. This alarming new development may be the result of human disturbance of natural habitats.

fewer shoots to the larvae. If the larvae are killed, then the shrubs eventually change their shape and assume a more tree-like growth form.

Pinyon pines are bisexual, carrying their male parts (strobili) on side shoots and the female cones at the tips of branches. Because the moth larvae prefer to feed at the tips of branches, heavily infested trees produce only strobili, female expression being suppressed.

The statistics of insect herbivory are impressive and underline the enormous influence they exert on whole ecosystems. The caterpillars of the mopane emperor moth, *Imbrasia belina*, are a good example. The caterpillars are called mopane worms and are an important human food in southern Africa (see Chapter 8). They feed on one of the dominant trees of the southern African veld, the mopane tree, *Colophospermum mopane*.

In 1993, a study carried out on a reserve of 4000 hectares (9884 acres) estimated that 19 million mopane worms ate 779 tonnes of leaves in six weeks. Their droppings amounted to 665 tonnes and are an important soil fertilizer. At 1993 prices, this was worth £161 000.

Elephants, greater kudu, impala, giraffes and other browsing animals also eat mopane trees. Elephants, in particular, have been blamed for widespread damage to this important tree, which sustains so much of animal life in the veld. Some conservationists have argued that elephants

BELOW: *Butterflies use their long, tubular tongues to feed on nectar from flowers. Often, as with this unnamed nymphalid from Argentina, they feed also at sap flows.*

RIGHT: *When not in use, a butterfly coils its proboscis under the head, as with this zebra butterfly,* Colobura dirce *(Trinidad).*

need to be culled in order to minimize the damage. This seems unfair, when the impact of mopane worms is taken into account.

The optimal number of elephants recommended by ecologists on the 4000-hectare site is 14. At this density, and if they only ate mopane leaves (which they don't), the elephants would take only 307 tonnes per year. This is less than half the amount eaten by mopane worms in six weeks. If mopane leaves represented only one-fifth of the elephant's intake, then their annual toll would be 61 tonnes, one-thirteenth of that eaten by the mopane worms.

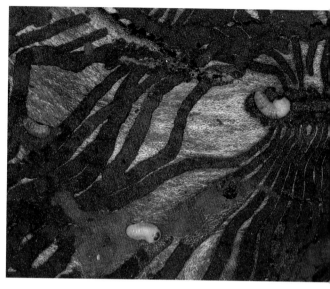

The feeding activities of the elm bark beetle, Scolytus scolytus, *result in these beautiful patterns. These beetles transmit the fungus which causes Dutch elm disease, which has destroyed many of the elm trees of Britain and Europe.*

The big difference between elephants and mopane worms is that elephants occasionally kill entire trees, while the mopane worms never do, even if they manage to defoliate a tree almost totally. Nevertheless, it is mopane worms which are responsible for the greatest consumption of leaves. And when they do cause defoliation, it is not the end of the world: if rain comes soon after the defoliation, then the trees burst into leaf again and this keeps the browsing animals in fodder to the end of winter. Not only do the mopane worms let the elephants off the hook, they also play a role in maintaining the food supply of many browsing mammals in the veld.

This is a dramatic example of just how vital it is for big-game ecologists to understand the keystone positions that insects occupy in sustaining ecosystems. For the sake of the big game that these ecologists are trying to conserve, it would be better if they became little-game ecologists and paid more attention to the myriad roles played by insects.

It may appear that herbivorous insects are bad news for plants but, in most natural situations, in the long term, there is an equilibrium, a balance between what insects take and what they return in the form of nutrients to the soil. Moreover, insectivorous birds, parasites and predatory insects normally keep the numbers of plant-eating insects sufficiently in check that the levels of damage to plants are sustainable.

One way in which plants respond to insect damage is to form growths around the feeding insects. These growths are called galls, and the feeding activities of the insects stimulates their formation. Galls may be found on roots, stems and leaves, and are responses to the larvae of beetles, flies and bugs, but by far the vast majority are caused by larvae of a special family of wasps, the cynipids.

Each gall involves a highly localized increase in cell size and number. Galls are particularly common on oak trees, *Quercus* spp., and typically a gall contains cell and tissue types not found elsewhere on the plant. Each gall is a truly unique response to a feeding insect, its form and structure being dependent on the insect species involved. Indeed, the uniqueness of the gall may be the result of DNA donated by the gall-inducing insect. Gall insects are among the most specialized of herbivores: each species feeds and develops on only one part, say a leaf bud or stem of one species of plant or a group of closely related species.

The advantage to the insect of spending its larval life in a gall is a rich source of special food cells in a protected environment. The outer layers of oak marble galls are chemically protected by tannins, and are so rich in these compounds that they were once a commercial source of tannin for the leather industry; they were also used in the manufacture of ink.

It is a matter of dispute as to whether the plant gains anything by expending energy on forming galls. It has been argued that the gall is a way of confining damage to an extremely localized area.

Some plants have changed the nature of their relationship with insects; it is as though it has become a case of 'If you can't beat them, then get them on your side', and the recruits are ants, mobilized as security guards. Most of these ant–plant associations are found in the tropics, but a very interesting one occurs in the south-eastern United States, involving the passion vine, *Passiflora incarnata*, and five species of nectar-greedy ants.

The passion vine produces nectar in its flowers in the normal way. But it also has nectaries situated in pairs on the stem of each leaf. The flowers secrete nectar only at specific times of the day, but these extra-floral nectaries are active continually and they attract a steady stream of ants which monopolize them.

The ants fuel their activities with nectar, and some of those activities include attacking beetles and grasshoppers, denying these insects access to leaves, buds and flowers. The ants have also been seen pruning away old leaves which had ceased to produce nectar.

Each of the five species of ants is active for a different period of the day, with little overlap between any two species. This means that the

OPPOSITE: *A final stage nymph of a bush cricket (katydid),* Macrocentron *sp. (Trinidad), eats a hibiscus leaf.*

THE BIRTH OF THE BEES

Once there was a time before bees. Then, in the Cretaceous period, about 90 million years ago, some hunting wasps got mixed up with the sex lives of plants: the stage was set for the evolution of bees.

The Cretaceous began 135 million years ago and ended some 65 million years before the present. It spanned the beginning of the end and then the final extinction of the dinosaurs; the evolutionary adventure which produced the mammals was well under way. And, also in the Cretaceous, the sexual needs of some groups of plants provided new dietary opportunities for flying insects.

In this time before bees, land plants relied on wind to carry pollen from the male parts of one plant to the female parts of another. If this lottery of sex-by-wind was to pay off, then plants had to produce vast amounts of pollen to ensure that at least some of it landed in the right place to bring about fertilization. Indeed, many primitive plants still persist with this lottery: when the male cones of pine trees are ripe, the slightest gust of wind releases smoky plumes of billions of pollen grains.

But it would not have been long before insects got in on the act. Pollen is highly nutritious; insects are opportunists. It is likely that many kinds of insects began to exploit pollen as food. In so doing, they would have accidentally transported pollen on their bodies from one plant to another and inadvertently subverted

the wind. And once this happened often enough, those plants with pollen-producing parts which were more attractive to insects than others would have had an advantage in reproduction. This differential in success is the essence of natural selection.

Selection will have ensured that plants continued to increase their attractiveness to insects. One way of doing this was to vary the menu on offer. Plants did this by providing nectar, a mixture of sugars. Thus, the plants now offered an energy-rich fuel to offset the energy expended by insects in flitting from plant to plant in search of protein-rich pollen.

So far, the word 'flower' has been avoided. This is

LEFT: *A queen bumblebee,* Bombus hortorum *(UK), uses her long tongue to probe the deep, tubular flower of a primrose,* Primula vulgaris.

ABOVE: *A female solitary bee,* Tetralonia malvae *(France), collects the large pollen grains from a mallow flower,* Malva *spp. This species specializes in collecting pollen from mallows. She compacts the pollen into a special brush of hairs, the scopa, on her hindlegs.*

because the flower as we know it did not exist until plants had added two more aids to their repertoire of ploys to recruit insects for sex by proxy: in a sea of green leaves, plants needed to advertise the whereabouts of their sexual parts. They began to broadcast on two channels of communication: sight and scent. Leaves close to or protecting the sex organs developed bright, eye-catching colours and shapes and became petals. Attractive scents were synthesized by special groups of cells situated on the petals or the sex organs. With the combination of petals and scents, true flowers were born: scents enable plants to announce their presence over long distances, while petals act as close-order cues for insects homing in on a rich food source.

One group of insects in particular adapted to the new food sources on offer by flowers. Members of a family of solitary hunting wasps, the Sphecidae, began to collect and store pollen instead of insect prey as food for their larvae. They developed branched body hairs, all the better to trap pollen grains, and special structures for the concentration and transport of pollen back to the nest. They also developed longer tongues, which enabled them to probe those flowers which sought to exclude all but the most efficient pollinators by evolving nectaries situated at the end of long, tubular flowers. In this way, bees were born.

Today, there are probably 30-40 000 species of bee. Most are solitary, that is, each nest is the work of a single female working alone, without the co-operation of a caste of workers.

The evolutionary history of bees is the history of an ever-specialized source of food And this had important implications for not only the apes which were our ancestors, but for us as well: about 30 per cent of our food is directly or indirectly dependent on the pollination services of bees. And it is one of the kindest coincidences of evolution that the scents attractive to bees also appeal to us, such very recent arrivals on the evolutionary scene.

ABOVE: *A female leafcutter bee,* Megachile willughbiella *(UK), forages at a thistle. Leafcutter bees line their nest cells with cut pieces of leaf and have the pollen scopa on the underside of the abdomen rather than the hindlegs.*

RIGHT: *Many plants have special mechanisms to ensure that pollen is placed accurately on a specific part of a bee's body. Here a male carpenter bee,* Xylocopa nigra *(Kenya), is neatly dusted on the back.*

An adult cicada, Brevisiana *spp. (Kenya), uses its sucking mouthparts to feed on tree sap. The tubular sucking apparatus is tough enough to penetrate bark.*

plant enjoys security patrols throughout daylight hours.

The importance of the ants to the passion vine can be demonstrated by a neat little experiment. If the extra-floral nectaries are removed, then the number of visiting ants declines rapidly and, at the same time, the rate of damage by leaf-chewing insects increases. Plants which enjoy the services of ant guards produce more fruit than unguarded ones.

It is cheaper for the passion vine to provide simple sugars in the form of nectar than to manufacture complex SPCs. It is cost-effective in another way: the plant needs only to produce just enough nectar to attract the minimum number of ants to be effective as guards. A symbiotic relationship with the ants has yet another pay-off: insect herbivores have demonstrated, time and again, that they can develop immunity to SPCs, but it is probably far more difficult for them to evolve defences against a mobile security force of stinging ants.

Old passion vines often have hollow stems, and these may become occupied by an ant colony. The plant therefore has its own resident security force, and this is reminiscent of a more sophisticated ant–plant symbiosis, found in Central and South America. Here, species of *Acacia* provide ants with nest sites in the form of hollow thorns.

As with the passion vine ants, these ants, species of *Pseudomyrmex*, keep the tree free of leaf-eating insects. They also remove fungal spores, pollen grains, spiders' webs, dust and any object which lands on the leaves. Even vines, which use the *Acacia* as a support, are killed by the ants: they bite a trough into the vine which encircles the stem, cutting off the flow of sap. The ants also afford protection from browsing deer and cattle. Even these large herbivores are stung if they come into contact with any part of the tree.

In return for these services, the *Acacia* provides not only a nest site, but also food in two forms: nectar, from extra-floral nectaries, and protein and oils from special structures called Beltian bodies. These grow at the tip of each leaflet and the ants harvest them, taking them back to their nest.

The importance of *Pseudomyrmex* ants to the *Acacia* trees can be demonstrated experimentally: removal of the ant colonies causes the tree to go into decline and it usually dies in three to twelve months. Not surprisingly, there is a species of ant which cheats on the arrangement. *Pseudomyrmex nigropilosa* invade *Acacia* trees which have lost their normal ant associates. They feed freely on the nectar and Beltian bodies provided by the tree, but make no attempt to protect it. In fact, if the tree is attacked, these parasitic ants run away and hide.

In Amazonian Brazil, there is another ant species, *Pseudomyrmex concolor*, which has a rather different relationship with the tree it protects. It nests in hollow leaves of the rainforest tree, *Tachigali myrmecophila*. The tree does provide food for the ants directly and the ants do not eat the herbivorous insects they attack. Instead, the tree harbours sap-sucking coccid bugs and the ants feed on the honeydew that they secrete. And the ants simply throw any attacking insects off the plant.

It seems that the tree is prepared to pay the price of supporting the coccids in order to remain attractive to the ants. The price is certainly right: trees which were experimentally deprived of ants for 18 months endured at least twice as much leaf loss as those with ants; leaves had their lives shortened by 50 per cent.

This is of crucial importance to the tree because of its lifestyle: it has a low growth rate and spends most of its life as a sapling in the shaded under-storey of the rainforest; it flowers and reproduces only once. For a tree such as this, permanently in the shade, the amount of leaf area available for photosynthesis can mean the difference between surviving long enough to flower and set seed, or dying before its single chance of reproduction. The defending force of ants ensures the tree of its longevity.

The feeding behaviour of ants plays an important role in plant protection in northern temperate forest. Here, wood ants, *Formica* spp., exert tremendous pressure on leaf-feeding insects. A normal-sized colony of *Formica polyctena* removes 6 million prey items in a year. A colony of the red wood ant, *F. rufa*, was monitored, and in one day brought in 21 700 caterpillars and sawfly larvae. For centuries, foresters in Central Europe have been using these ants as control agents against defoliating insects.

CARNIVORES

If insects seem to be busy eating the world's plants, they are also busy eating each other: the worst enemies of insects are other insects.

Carnivorous insects fall into two main categories: active predators and sit-and-wait strategists.

Active predators

Active predators include nocturnal ground beetles and tiger beetles. Ground beetles run around in leaf litter, forest floors and pasturelands at night, preying on insect larvae and roosting adult insects. In contrast, tiger beetles have good all-round vision and actively chase insect prey on bare, open ground or in sand dunes, in broad daylight.

Many bush crickets (katydids) are carnivores, such as the European oak bush cricket, *Meconema thalassinum*. They creep about among vegetation and pounce on any small insects they encounter. Earwigs, too, will take insect prey. Although known to gardeners as a pest of plants, the common earwig, *Forficula auricularia*, preys also on small insects. Two oriental earwig species are rather more specialized: *Xeniaria jacobseni* and *Arixenia esau* both live in bat roosts in caves, where they feed on skin debris and secretions of the bats.

The most impressive active predators are hawker dragonflies. They patrol regular beats, often flying considerable distances from the ponds and rivers in which they breed. They take insects on the wing, using their powerful jaws to dismember prey, while holding it with their long spiny legs. Dragonflies often follow groups of grazing mammals, and feed on the insects that are disturbed as the animals make their way across country.

The dragonflies' more delicate relatives, the damselflies, rarely stray far from water; they tend to patrol the weedy margins of ponds and rivers, feeding mainly on flies.

An exception, though, is the giant tropical species, *Megaloprepus coerulatus*, which feeds in an unusual and highly specialized way. This damselfly hovers in front of the large orb webs made by large *Nephila* spiders. From the web it plucks much smaller spiders which feed sneakily on the insect prey caught there. It is mostly the male damselflies which show this behaviour; after snatching their prey, they fly to nearby vegetation to eat it.

OPPOSITE: *A red damselfly,* Pyrrhosoma nymphula *(UK), flew into the web of a spider,* Argiope sp.*, and was temporarily trapped. Here it has seized the spider as prey and backs out of the web.*

THE FLYING STILETTOS

Many insects with piercing and sucking mouthparts have adopted a predatory diet and feed on the body fluids of other insects: assassin bugs, shieldbugs and robberflies all make a living in this way. Typically, they pierce the body of their victim through the soft, flexible membranes between the cuticular plates, and inject saliva. This paralyses the prey and then digests the victim's tissues. The predator then sucks up the resulting nutritious liquid.

Some predatory suckers have taken things one step further and specialize on the blood of vertebrates: amphibia, reptiles, birds and mammals. The saliva of these insects – assassin bugs, mosquitoes, midges,

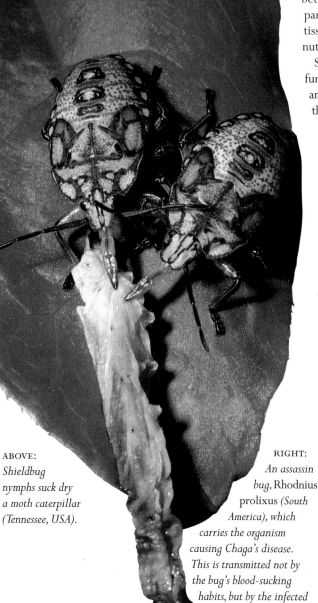

ABOVE:
Shieldbug nymphs suck dry a moth caterpillar (Tennessee, USA).

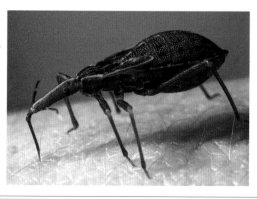

RIGHT:
An assassin bug, Rhodnius prolixus *(South America), which carries the organism causing Chaga's disease. This is transmitted not by the bug's blood-sucking habits, but by the infected faeces of the insect.*

tsetse flies — contains anti-coagulants, which, when injected, ensure that the victim's blood does not clot for the duration of the meal.

With the evolution of blood-sucking came the evolution of specialized disease organisms which spend part of their developmental life-history in the body of the blood-sucking insect, part in the body of the insect's hosts. Thus came malaria, transmitted by *Anopheles* mosquitoes, yellow fever, transmitted by *Aëdes* mosquitoes, and sleeping sickness, transmitted by tsetse flies, *Glossina* spp. In addition, there are at least 80 different virus diseases where human-biting flies are the vectors.

LEFT: *Acute eyesight and aerial acrobatics have enabled this robberfly,* Promachus *spp. (Kenya), to catch a worker honeybee,* Apis mellifera, *on the wing. Small milichiid flies lap up the bee's body fluids leaking from the wound.*

RIGHT: *Already distended with blood, a tsetse fly,* Glossina morsitans *(Kenya), feeds on human blood. Species of* Glossina *transmit the organism which causes sleeping sickness. One in six of the world's human population is infected with an insect-transmitted disease.*

ABOVE: *Another hapless honeybee has fallen prey, this time to an assassin bug,* Apiomeris *spp. (Mexico). Once again, milichiid flies, too small to catch their own prey, lap up liquids oozing from the wound.*

Sit-and-wait strategists

BELOW: *Feeding in a dragonfly larva. Top: at rest, head in side view with mask retracted. Bottom: the mask extends to grasp prey, which is impaled on claws and then brought back to within reach of the jaws.*

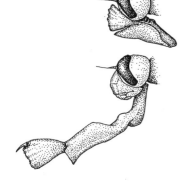

Sit-and-wait strategists have lightning responses to any insect prey which comes within their acute visual field. Examples are the aquatic larvae of dragonflies and damselflies, adult darter dragonflies, pond skaters, robberflies and praying mantids.

The aquatic larvae are well camouflaged and sit still on the bottom of ponds and rivers. They have a remarkable structure, the mask, so called because when the insect is at rest it covers the rest of the mouthparts. The mask is a device for seizing prey and bringing it within reach of the jaws. It is a hinged unit (see diagram left), armed with a pair of movable hooks.

The larva remains motionless for much of the time, until its stereoscopic eyes detect prey. Then, the larva stalks it slowly until it is within range of the mask. This extends, impales the prey on the hooks and then folds back into position in 25-thousandths of a second. This rapid extension is initiated by powerful contractions of abdominal muscles which send a rush of blood into the mask; retraction is under direct muscular control and brings the prey within reach of the jaws.

Dragonfly larvae have catholic tastes: worms, crustacea, tadpoles and fish are all fair game for these opportunistic hunters.

RIGHT: *The larva of a large hawker dragonfly,* Aeshna *sp. (UK), has used its lightning-quick mask to capture a stickleback and bring it to within reach of its massive jaws.*

Unlike hawker dragonflies, adult darter dragonflies perch on some prominent vantage point such as the tip of a branch and launch themselves into the air when suitable flying prey attracts their attention. As with the hawker dragonflies, they capture insect prey on the wing.

A robberfly or asilid has a similar perching habit, often on large thorns or the barbs of barbed wire fencing. It, too, darts out at any suitable prey, which it grasps with its spiny legs and takes back to a perch. Here, the robberfly sinks its piercing proboscis into a chink in the insect's armour plating and injects digestive enzymes before imbibing a liquidized meal.

Robberflies often catch prey which are well protected with a sting. However, the lightning responses of the fly are too much for worker wasps or honeybees.

Pond skaters, *Gerris* spp., have an interesting way of detecting prey. Sometimes called water-striders or wherrymen, they sit on the surface film of ponds, supported by pads of dense hair on the middle and hind pairs of legs; their forelegs are used in manipulating prey. When an insect falls into the water, the ripples set up by its struggles are detected by special detectors in the pond skater's legs. Sensors detect the time differences between ripples hitting different legs; this is processed

Attracted by surface-borne vibrations from a struggling fly, a water strider or pond skater, Gerris *sp. (USA), now uses its sucking mouthparts to make a meal of the fly's body fluids.*

to give directional data and the pond skater homes in on the prey.

Sometimes several will home in on an insect much larger than themselves, such as a female damselfly laying eggs in water weeds. They jointly overcome her struggles, insert their piercing and sucking mouthparts into her body and inject digestive enzymes; they then feed on the resulting partially liquefied tissues. Pond skaters sometimes attack and eat small fish which come to the surface.

The masters of sit-and-wait strategy are the 1800 species of praying mantids. Endowed with stereoscopic vision as acute as any in the insect world, a mantis is a formidable killing and eating machine. Its front legs are raptorial, that is, adapted for seizing and holding on to prey, being armed with large, sharp, backwardly directed spines.

Praying mantids are so called because when in their sitting and waiting phase, they hold up their raptorial front legs in what seems to be an attitude of prayer. Mantids are extremely good at sitting still for long periods and, because the compound eyes of insects are highly sensitive to movement, a motionless mantid is effectively invisible to any passing insect.

Mantids have very mobile heads; when one spots an insect, it remains motionless, but turns its head so that it looks at the prey directly. Then, in 30- to 50-thousandths of a second, the mantis reaches out, grasps the prey and brings it within reach of its jaws. Most prey are insects, but mantids often take frogs and small lizards as well.

Raptorial front legs similar to those of mantids have independently evolved in mantispid lacewings and some assassin bugs, all voracious predators of other insects.

BELOW: *Evolved quite independently from those of mantids, the raptorial legs of this assassin bug,* Amulius longiceps *(Malaysia), serve the same prey grasping and holding purposes.*

OMNIVORES AND SCAVENGERS

Although most herbivorous insects show some degree of host-plant specialization, there are some which will feed on a wide range of plant species. A notable example is the Chinese wax scale insect, *Ceroplastes sinensis*, a sap-sucking bug. This has been recorded from 200 species of plants in at least 50 families.

Cockroaches are true omnivores, feeding on almost any organic matter. This is one reason they have been so successful at invading our houses: even the most well-ordered of households has tiny scraps of food lost and forgotten behind kitchen cupboards and other nooks and

OPPOSITE: *A female praying mantis,* Acontista *spp. (Trinidad), eats a fly. Biting and chewing mouthparts, combined with lightning reflexes and spiny, grasping front legs, make praying mantids efficient killing machines.*

ABOVE: *Fire ants, Solenopsis sp. (Florida), scavenge on the remains of a dead corn snake.*

BELOW: *A scavenging denizen of tropical dry forest, the hissing cockroach, Elliptorhina javanica (Madagascar), is so called because, when disturbed, it deters predators with a sudden loud hiss produced by the forcible expulsion of air from the second pair of abdominal spiracles (breathing pores). More subdued hissing is used in courtship.*

crannies. Several species, such as the American cockroach, *Periplaneta americana*, have become almost cosmopolitan, having followed human migrations around the globe. Cockroaches have rightly been called the insect equivalents of rats and mice.

Cockroaches often act as true scavengers, eating dead insects, including members of their own species. The eating habits of cockroaches blur the distinction between omnivory and scavenging, but some insects make a specialist living as scavengers.

Scavenger flies, such as *Tetanocera hyalipennis*, eat the remains of insects discarded from their webs by spiders. Scorpionflies (Mecoptera) feed on dead and injured insects. The common European scorpionfly, *Panorpa communis*, often scavenges the remains of insects in spiders' webs and usually manages to do so without attracting the fatal attention of the spider. If a *Panorpa* accidentally blunders into a spider's web, however, then it usually falls prey to the alerted spider.

P. communis most frequently scavenges on the semi-liquid remains of flies which have been killed by an entomophagous (insect-eating) fungus. The fungus does not attack the *Panorpa*: it is dangerous only to its own specific host.

Many insects specialize in scavenging the dead bodies of vertebrates. There is a distinct succession of flies, beetles and moths which visit a body, the order of visitation matching the stages of decomposition.

In relatively dry conditions, one of the last stages of decay is the mummification of skin and sinews. The final processing of this apparently unpromising food is the work of the larvae of tineid moths (clothes moths) and dermestid beetles. Both moths and beetles also scavenge on skin debris and shed feathers and hairs in the nests and dens of birds and mammals. For the moths, it was a short step to enter our houses, where we provide them with a bonanza in the form of woollen clothes: as far as the moths are concerned, a wardrobe is a super den. And dermestid beetles, especially species

About 100 larvae of a parasitoid wasp, Cotesia *spp., have spent their lives eating inside the caterpillars of a tobacco hornworm moth,* Manduca sexta *(North America). Originating from eggs injected by their mother, the larvae have burst out and spun silk cocoons in which they will pupate.*

of *Anthrenus*, have invaded our natural history museums, where, if we are not careful, their larvae eat prized specimens of bird skins and insect collections.

Some scavengers are extremely specialized. For example, relatives of the pond skaters live on the surface of the sea, hundreds of miles from land. These ocean striders, *Hylobates* spp., are found in warm seas and are distributed where ocean currents concentrate masses of surface flotsam of organic origin. Here the *Hylobates* scavenge on dead insects which have been washed out to sea, and the occasional dead sea bird.

Perhaps the most bizarre scavengers are tiny milichiid flies, *Desmometopa* spp. They congregate wherever there are spiders, assassin bugs and robberflies. As these predators feed on their prey, the little flies lap up the body fluids leaking from the wounds. The flies are too small to be of interest to the much larger predators.

FEEDING BY TRICKERY

Some predatory insects have evolved very sophisticated ploys to lure insect prey to their doom. One smart operator is the rove beetle, *Leistotrophus versicolor*, which lives in the forests of Central America. It resembles a piece of dung and is a specialist predator on adult flies; it lurks on dung or carrion and pounces on flies attracted to such food. In the absence of these resources, the beetle settles on a leaf or rock and deposits a secretion which smells of dung. It then positions itself with its head above the droplet and waits for small flies to be lured by this bait.

Another form of bizarre subterfuge is operated by a South American assassin bug, *Salyavata variegata*. Like many of its relatives, it sticks debris over its body, so that it no longer looks like an insect. It lives on the nests of termites, *Nasutitermes* spp., and the camouflaging debris on its body makes it look like part of the nest material.

The bug eats termites, sucking them dry with its proboscis after injecting digestive juices. When it has finished dealing with a termite in this way, it leaves the victim impaled on the proboscis and then pokes it into one of the nest entrances. Other termite workers come to investigate, smell one of their own kind and are unperturbed by the presence of the bug, until one of them falls prey and is destined to become the next bait.

Eerie glowing lights are used by the larvae of Australian and New Zealand fungus gnats, *Arachnocampa* spp., to catch small flies. Each larva secretes a beaded, sticky thread, suspended from the roof of the cave which is its home. The beads are luminescent and attract small flies, which stick to the thread. The gnat larvae climb down and eat them.

RIGHT: *Larvae of the fungus gnat,* Arachnocampa flava *(Australia), have a bizarre way of catching flying insect prey. These luminous grubs secrete long threads with sticky beads of luminous fluid arranged along their length, suspended from vegetation or the roof of a cave. These attract night-flying insects, which become stuck to the threads and fall prey to the gnat larva.*

A female ichneumon wasp, Grotea sp. (Costa Rica), uses her ovipositor to inject eggs through the tough mud nest of a social wasp, Montezuma sp. Her larvae will feed on those of the host.

DOING WITHOUT FOOD

Although it is clear by now that insects are adept at finding and exploiting food, there are times in the lives of many of them when they have no choice but to fast.

In northern, temperate regions, the queens of social wasps and bumblebees hibernate through the winter. They depend on stored fat to sustain them then. In fact, they spend more than 50 per cent of their one-year life in hibernation.

Fleas are particularly good at fasting. Species which parasitize migratory birds have to be able to withstand a foodless winter in their hosts' nest until they return the following spring. The human flea, *Pulex irritans*, can withstand 125 days without food, an adaptation evolved to cope with the semi-nomadic lifestyles of our cave-dwelling ancestors.

Insects have evolved a dazzling array of intricate and elegant ways of finding and exploiting food, ways of coping with plenty and famine. This has made them the dominant life forms on this planet.

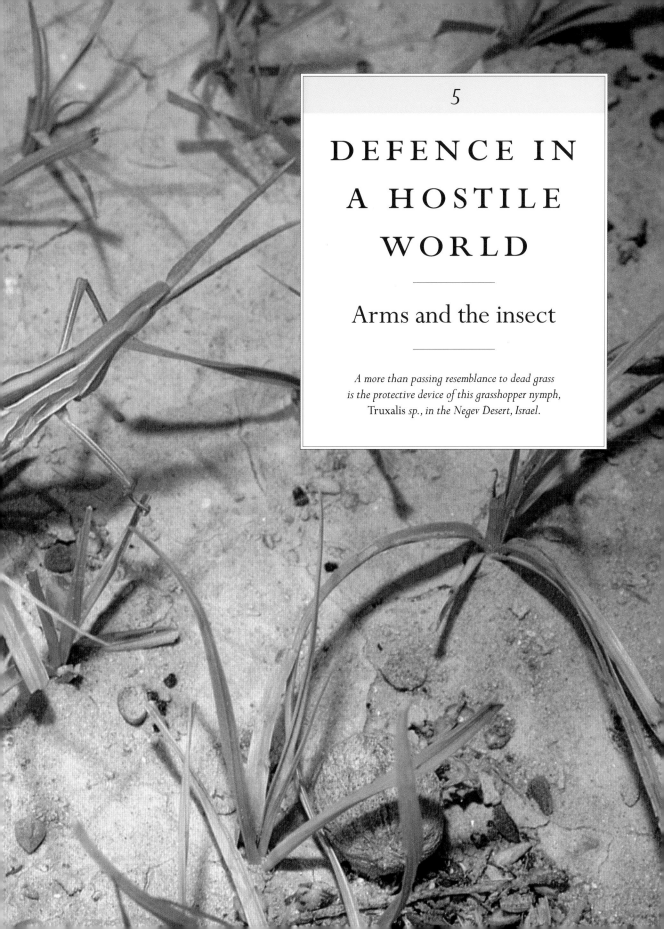

5

DEFENCE IN A HOSTILE WORLD

Arms and the insect

*A more than passing resemblance to dead grass
is the protective device of this grasshopper nymph,
Truxalis sp., in the Negev Desert, Israel.*

Insects are such prominent members of nearly all terrestrial habitats that it is no surprise that they are a major food resource for other animals. We saw in the last chapter that in terms of numbers of species, the insects' worst enemies are other insects. But in terms of numbers of insects eaten, frogs, toads, lizards, lizards and birds may rival the predatory insects. And insects have arrived at a seemingly endless number of defensive ploys against these enemies.

MECHANICAL DEFENCE

A protective resemblance to lichen-covered bark is a defensive ploy of this unnamed bush cricket (katydid), a denizen of cloud forest in Costa Rica. Any predator which sees through the ploy can expect a second line of defence: a prickly mouthful and a bitter taste.

Many insects, especially large tropical bush crickets (katydids) and beetles, rely on tough thick cuticle as their main defence against the probing beaks of birds or the jaws of lizards. To this armour plating, many add noxious chemicals as a second line of defence (see page 138). And strong jaws or stabbing mouthparts can also be mobilized: anyone foolish enough to handle the common water boatman, *Notonecta glauca*, will feel a sharp stabbing pain as the insect jabs its stiletto-like proboscis into the hand, injecting burning digestive juices.

A threatening display is another ploy, often used by praying mantids,

which rear up, brandishing their spiny raptorial legs in an aggressive posture. They can easily draw blood if mishandled.

A few insects indulge in death-feigning (thanatosis) as a means of escape from predators. This is common among leaf-feeding weevils, which, when disturbed, retract their legs and drop off the plant.

SENSORY AWARENESS

Acute eyesight and lightning responses get many an insect out of trouble. This is especially true of flies; only chameleons and the most adroit of birds can catch them.

Many insects have a sense of hearing, usually involved in courtship (see Chapter 6), but some have a sense of hearing for reasons of self-preservation. Some praying mantids, bush crickets (katydids), lacewings and moths have ears which are tuned into the ultra-sonic frequencies emitted by insectivorous bats. They are sensitive to bat calls in the frequency range 30–100 kHz. Once such an insect realizes it has been picked up on the bat's radar, it takes evasive action and falls to the ground, out of radar range.

OVERLEAF: *A South African bush cricket (katydid),* Armativentris *spp., adds spines to its armour. It also has chemical defence, in the form of a foul-tasting yellow liquid, seen here exuding from glands between the armour plating.*

BELOW: *Large eyes and lightning reflexes make this predatory water bug, a backswimmer,* Anisops *sp. (Australia), a formidable predator. But they also afford protection from other predators.*

PROTECTIVE RESEMBLANCE
AND CAMOUFLAGE

One way of avoiding being eaten is not to be seen. For this reason, many insects such as ground beetles, earwigs and moths are active only at night. By day, they roost under stones, in bark crevices, in leaf litter or under leaves.

More sophisticated ways of not being seen involve being around during the day but being virtually invisible. Many insects, from a very broad range of insect groups, have adopted protective resemblance as their main means of defence. They resemble, often uncannily, inanimate objects, or, from the predator's point of view, inedible objects. Thus, many insects look like stones, seeds, dead grass, broken sticks, thorns or a bird dropping.

Some insects, particularly bush crickets (katydids), but also mantids and bugs, resemble leaves. This resemblance is not just in shape and

BELOW: *This caterpillar of an unnamed noctuid moth (Costa Rica) mimics a bird dropping.*

RIGHT: *This bush cricket (katydid),* Phylloptera *sp. (Brazil), resembles a living green leaf.*

OPPOSITE: *Tree hoppers,* Umbonia spinosa *(Venezuela), arrange themselves along a stem, capitalizing on their resemblance to thorns.*

HOW NOT TO BE SEEN

Insects have evolved very many ways of not being seen. Whatever visual ploy a particular species uses, sitting still for most of the time and moving only very slowly is part of the trick of concealment: birds and lizards have acute vision and are likely to notice if a stone or dead leaf gets up and walks around.

The uncanny protective resemblances of these insects to a wide range of objects in the natural environment,

shown here, is ample testimony to the fine tuning of natural selection. And the principal agents of selection were, and are, birds and lizards. Although many insects prey on other insects, it is unlikely that they played much of a role here. The kinds of visual tricks used by insects which protect themselves in this way are effective with the eyes of vertebrates, like our own, rather than with the compound eyes of insects.

BELOW: *The caterpillar of this unnamed arctiid moth (Madagascar) resembles the lichen background on which it feeds.*

RIGHT: *A grasshopper,* Trachypetrella *sp., resembles a quartzite stone in the Namaqualand desert of South Africa.*

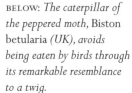

BELOW: *The caterpillar of the peppered moth,* Biston betularia *(UK), avoids being eaten by birds through its remarkable resemblance to a twig.*

RIGHT: *This bug,* Phyllomorpha laciniata *(Israel), is superbly protected by its close resemblance to the everlasting plant,* Paronychia *sp., on which it feeds.*

LEFT: *The nymph of the praying mantis,* Phyllocrania illudens *(Madagascar), escapes predators by its wonderful resemblance to a shrivelled dead leaf.*

RIGHT: *A thorn-bug,* Umbonia crassicornis *(Florida), next to a rose thorn, which it resembles so closely.*

False head markings and false antennae at the tip of the hindwings of this moth, Lirimiris sp. (Costa Rica), direct the pecks of hungry birds to a non-vital part of the body.

colour: it also extends to the pattern of veins and the mottlings of fungus attack.

Other leaf mimics specialize in looking like curled-up, brown, dead leaves. To add to the effect, some species dangle off a twig by one leg and twist slowly, as though being moved by a breeze. The dead-leaf mimicking mantis from South America, *Acanthops falcata*, is a good example.

Also effective is the caterpillar of the silver king shoemaker butterfly, *Prepona antimache*, also from South America. It resembles a crinkled, dead leaf and suspends itself by a silk thread from the tip of a green, living leaf. In so doing, it resembles a type of leaf decay which is common among tropical trees, where death of the leaf and withering proceed from the tip of the leaf towards the base.

Other leaf mimics include insect damage as part of their repertoire of trickery. Thus, some Malaysian tussock moths, *Carniola* spp., have

LEFT: *Many moths and butterflies have independently evolved false head mimicry as a defence against bird predation, as with this zebra butterfly from Trinidad,* Colobura dirce.

transparent patches in their otherwise scale-covered wings, resembling one particular pattern of leaf damage caused by insects. The moth's own wing veins are visible in the clear patches of wing and the overall effect is of a dead leaf which has been partially skeletonized. And when at rest, with its wings folded vertically to expose the undersides, the leaf shoemaker butterfly of Central and South America, *Anea itis*, resembles a dead or dying leaf with ragged margins, where pieces have been bitten away by leafcutter ants. It also has localized mottlings which resemble fungal damage.

Another way of being invisible is to resemble the background. Many insects employ camouflage and have modified not only their colour but also surface texturing and bodily postures to enhance the overall effect.

Lichen-covered bark is a common background, and such groups as cicadas, shieldbugs, bush crickets (katydids) and moth caterpillars have species which resemble encrusting lichens.

OVERLEAF: *An uncanny resemblance to dead leaves is the remarkable defensive ploy of this stick insect,* Phyllium bioculatum *(New Guinea).*

THE EYES HAVE IT

A wide range of insects have evolved eyespots on their wings. Apart from those illustrated here, eyespots are found in praying mantids and moth caterpillars.

Insect eyespots have several features in common, including concentric circles which resemble the iris and pupils of a real eye, and off-centre pale patches; the latter give the impression of glints from large eyes.

Birds are deterred by large eyes, especially if the pair they encounter on the hindwings of an insect are widely separated: this gives the impression of a large head and muzzle, something to be avoided.

The golden emperor moth,
Loepa katincka *(India).*

Eyespots are often found on the hindwings of insects which are well camouflaged, in which case they are normally hidden by the cryptic forewings. The eyespots are suddenly exposed in a startle display if a curious bird has penetrated the insect's first line of defence, namely, camouflage. Eyespots, then, are a second line of defence.

In small insects, eyespots are not always very accurate depictions of eyes and here their main function may be to deflect a pecking bird away from vital to less vital parts of the body.

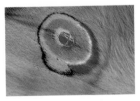

The royal oak silkmoth,
Antheraea roylei *(India).*

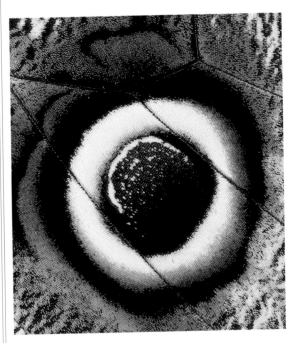

ABOVE: *An owl butterfly,* Caligo eurilochus *(Costa Rica). Here, the concentric rings and highlights give the impression of a real, shining eye, with a pupil.*

RIGHT: *Peanut bugs,* Laternaria laternaria *(Costa Rica), one of which has been startled and has suddenly exposed the eyespots on the hindwings in a defensive flash display.*

LEFT: *The zigzag emperor moth,* Gonimbrasia tyrrhea *(Zambia). Eyespots have evolved independently in many groups of insects, especially the moths and butterflies.*

BELOW: *Another emperor moth,* Reucanella leucane *(Mexico).*

CHEMICAL DEFENCE

Most of us have had experience with the chemical defences of insects: wasps and bees pack a sting with which they inject venom. The venom is a complex mixture of chemicals, each with a specially designed end result. Some chemicals cause pain, others induce swelling and yet others depress the blood pressure; there is usually one which induces changes in the victim's tissues which make it easier for the other components to spread. Even those ants and bees which are stingless are not without chemical protection. The ants can mobilize a pungent, temporarily blinding spray of formic acid, and some stingless bees produce a corrosive, blistering secretion from glands in the head.

Residents of certain leafy suburbs may be familiar with another example of chemical warfare waged by insects. Caterpillars of the brown-tail moth, *Euproctis chrysorrhoea*, have a dense clothing of hairs. Each hair is hollow and connected to a cuticular gland. This secretes an irritant; if these hairs brush against one's skin, they break off and a nasty, blistering rash occurs. Because the larvae live gregariously on ornamen-

A caterpillar of the black swallowtail butterfly, Papilio polyxenes *(USA), has everted its forked osmeterium, a double-edged line of defence: the sudden eversion of this brightly coloured gland serves to startle a would-be predator or parasitic wasp, but, if this does not work, the unpleasant scent emitted by this gland may do the trick.*

tal trees grown in towns, they can be a real problem, especially because of a neat adaptation of this species: when a larva pupates and spins its silken cocoon, the irritant hairs of the caterpillar are incorporated into the outer layers of silk. Later, when the adult moths have vacated the cocoons, the tattered remains may be blown about, releasing hairs into the air. These windborne hairs can cause severe eye irritations in people living in urban areas where the moth has been very common.

While the caterpillars of the brown-tail moth incorporate its defensive hairs into its cocoon, the economical use of defensive resources does not stop here. When a female moth emerges from her cocoon, she picks up bunches of the irritant hairs from the cocoon with a dense brush of hairs at the tip of her abdomen. She sheds these over her eggs during laying, so that they too are protected.

The caterpillars of a South American emperor moth have even more dangerous hairs. The glands which supply them secrete a powerful anticoagulant: contact with these larvae can therefore result in severe haemorrhages and sometimes death from loss of blood.

The chemical defences of ants, wasps, bees and the brown-tail moth are all manufactured by the insects themselves. Other deployers of home-grown chemical weaponry are many bugs, which give off unpleasant scents when disturbed, and many beetles. Some rove beetles, *Paederus* spp., are particularly well protected. They produce a highly noxious liquid which causes severe blistering. The active agent is a chemical called paederin and, if this gets into the eyes, it can cause blindness through acute ulceration of the cornea.

The famous Spanish fly is, in fact, a beetle, *Lytta vesicatoria*. Its wing cases are packed with a chemical, cantharidin, which causes very unpleasant blistering. The alleged aphrodisiac properties of this beetle depend on the chemical causing a mild, supposedly pleasant and therefore erotically stimulating effect on the lining of the urethra during urination. Unfortunately, it is virtually impossible to control the dosage when eating the dried wing cases of *Lytta*, so, more often than not, what was intended as an induction of erotic ecstasy leads to a visit to a urologist. Nevertheless, there are legitimate uses for cantharidin in the preparation of drugs for more mundane uses.

This caterpillar of an unnamed limacodid moth (Java), is armed with hollow, defensive spines which contain a stinging fluid.

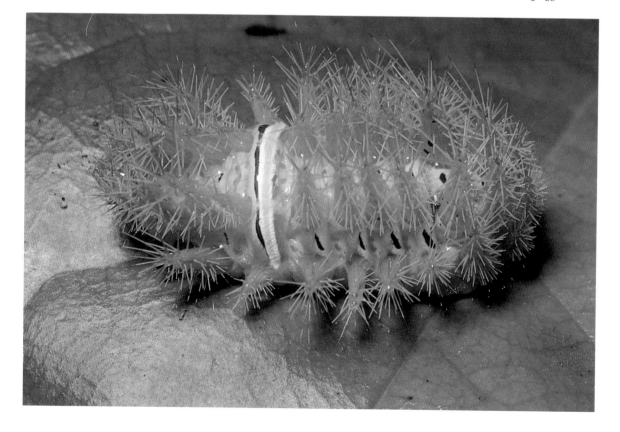

Less spectacular in effect, but more dramatic in appearance, is a strange form of defence found in the larvae and adults of ladybird beetles (ladybugs). If disturbed by a predator, the ladybird suddenly bleeds from special weak areas in the joints of its legs, releasing an extremely bitter-tasting, bright orange-yellow blood. This is called reflex bleeding. The insects seem able to withstand this loss of blood, and it is thought that birds learn to associate the bright colour with a very nasty taste and avoid ladybirds in the future.

The body fluids of some beetles are extremely toxic. In South Africa, the indigenous hunters of the Kalahari Desert use the fluid from the crushed bodies of *Diamphidia nigroarrata* as lethal arrow poison. Their quarry is killed by general paralysis.

Other beetles provide a literally explosive experience for any predator foolish enough to tackle them. These are the famous bombardier ground beetles, mainly *Brachinus* spp., found in North America and Europe.

When attacked, the beetle releases from the anus, at a temperature of 100°C, a jet of *p*-benzoquinone. This chemical is highly repugnant to spiders, predatory insects, rodents and birds. The release is accompanied by an audible pop, like the crackle of gunfire. The beetles have a highly mobile tip to the abdomen, so they can direct their line of fire at the predator.

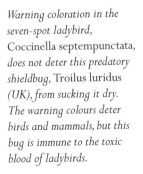

Warning coloration in the seven-spot ladybird, Coccinella septempunctata, *does not deter this predatory shieldbug,* Troilus luridus *(UK), from sucking it dry. The warning colours deter birds and mammals, but this bug is immune to the toxic blood of ladybirds.*

P-benzoquinone is volatile and unstable, so the beetles cannot store it; instead, they manufacture it, explosively, on demand, at the time of need. Paired glands synthesize and store a mixture of hydrogen peroxide and quinones. When attacked, the beetle discharges the mixture into a combustion chamber via a one-way valve. This chamber contains oxidizing enzymes, which catalyse the explosive formation of *p*-benzoquinone. The force of the explosion closes the one-way valve and in this way the chemical spray is forcibly discharged through the anus.

Very many insects do not make their own chemical weapons; they obtain them from the plants they feed on. We saw in Chapter 4 that many plants have evolved chemical defences of their own and these deter herbivorous insects. But many insects have subverted this and are either immune to the plant poisons or modify them chemically and, in either case, store them in their tissues. This renders them unpalatable to vertebrate predators such as lizards and birds. Species which sequester and use plant chemicals in this way are found among beetles, grasshoppers and, particularly, butterflies and moths.

Such insects advertise their distastefulness with patterns of bright, conspicuous colours. Bands and spots of orange, red, yellow, black and white are common. Predators learn to associate such patterns with a distasteful or emetic experience and thus avoid such insects subsequently.

Some warningly coloured moths, such as the garden tiger, *Arctia caja*, have an additional defensive ploy. By day, they roost, sometimes in prominent places, but are protected by their warning coloration. They fly by night, when a conspicuous pattern of bright colours is no protection against bats. Instead, they can hear the ultra-sonic sounds which constitute the bats' radar system; they respond with sounds of their own which deter the bats, perhaps by jamming the radar system.

The evolution of warning coloration paved the

ABOVE: The warning colours of this nymph of the grasshopper, Tropidacris cristatus *(Costa Rica), signals to would-be predators that it makes a foul-tasting mouthful.*

BELOW: Two forms of defence: nymphs of the bug Libyaspis coccinelloides *(Madagascar), use cryptic coloration to escape detection, while the adults use a very different strategy: they are brightly, warningly coloured to advertise their distasteful nature.*

MODELS AND MIMICS: BATESIAN MIMICRY

The great Victorian naturalist, Henry Bates, was the first to suggest that distasteful, warningly coloured insects may have their colour patterns copied by species which are not chemically protected. The mimicry system which now bears his name was based on his observations of tropical butterflies, and Batesian mimicry is now known in many insect groups in many parts of the world. The toxic species are called models and the non-toxic species with the same livery as the model are called mimics.

Bates speculated that distasteful or poisonous butterflies are always marked with bright, eye-catching patterns of colour and, through painful experience,

birds learn to associate these colours with unpleasant effects, such as a foul taste and/or vomiting. Being temporarily disabled in this way may have dire consequences for a bird which is rearing chicks: a delay in the supply of food may threaten their survival. Birds, then, have very good reasons to learn quickly that certain kinds of insects should be avoided.

Warning colours are a direct channel of communication between insect and bird, with a clear, unequivocal message: 'Don't eat me or you'll be sorry!' The fact that birds do get the message has been amply demonstrated experimentally, with birds being offered harmless insects or food items which have been brightly

ABOVE: *The warning colours of this butterfly,* Acraea macaria hemileuca *(Kenya), indicate this is a poisonous species. It is a model for a non-toxic species...*

...the swallowtail butterfly, Papilio jacksoni (RIGHT), *which mimics the* Acraea. *When a non-toxic species mimics the warning colour pattern of a toxic species, this is called Batesian mimicry.*

marked with food dyes. Experienced birds avoid this food, while naive birds eat it. If the naive birds are then given distasteful food which is also brightly coloured, they soon learn to associate the colours with an unpleasant experience and avoid it.

Some non-toxic insects have plugged into the channel of communication established by the toxic species and started broadcasting false messages on the same wavelength. Under the pressures exerted by predatory birds, those non-toxic species (mimics) which had some general resemblance to toxic ones (models) had a better chance of survival than those which did not. Over time and in each of millions of successive generations, the birds 'selected out' those mimics which looked least like the models. In this way, natural selection arrived at the remarkable and close resemblances between mimics and models shown here.

For the system to work, mimic and model must share the same habitat and periods of seasonal activity. The model must also walk a chemical tightrope: it should be sufficiently noxious to be a memorable experience, but not so toxic as to kill the birds, otherwise they would have no chance to learn. And the dynamics of the whole are directly dependent on the visual acuity of birds, their memory capabilities and their ability to generalize.

ABOVE: *This oil beetle,* Mylabris oculata *(South Africa), is chemically protected by the presence of a powerful poison in the wing cases. The conspicuous markings are a warning to would-be predators, but this signal is subverted by...*

...this jewel beetle, Agelia petali *(*RIGHT*) which is a Batesian mimic of the oil beetle.*

COMMON CAUSE: MÜLLERIAN MIMICRY

Named after Fritz Müller, the nineteenth-century naturalist who first detected it, Müllerian mimicry does not involve the association of chemically protected models and innocuous mimics. Instead, it is an association of species, all of which are distasteful and in which all members of the complex have a similar pattern of warning coloration.

As with Batesian mimicry, pressure from predatory birds is the driving force behind Müllerian mimicry. It pays distasteful species which share a habitat to transmit a common message – the same as the models' in Batesian mimicry: 'Don't eat me or you'll be sorry!' But, in this case, all transmitters are telling the truth.

The advantage with Müllerian mimicry is that birds have to remember only one pattern of warning coloration, and thus fewer insects are damaged or killed during a bird's learning process. Moreover, secondary reinforcement may operate: a predator's avoidance of the noxious species is strengthened by seeing its warning pattern, without the bird needing to taste it.

Müllerian mimicry involves very close resemblance between, sometimes, quite unrelated species, as shown here. This kind of mimicry is found in butterflies, moths, beetles, wasps and bees.

With both Batesian and Müllerian mimicry, the process of a bird's learning inevitably involves the deaths of some insects, but it has been shown that many warningly coloured, toxic insects have tougher than usual cuticle. This means that some, at least, may survive being pecked at by birds and live to be a flying emetic another day.

A Müllerian assemblage of distasteful or poisonous species which have evolved the same patterns of warning coloration:
ABOVE LEFT: *a sweet oil butterfly,* Mechanitis isthmia *(Trinidad).*
ABOVE RIGHT: *a helicon butterfly,* Heliconius isabella *(Trinidad).*
LEFT: *a nymphalid butterfly,* Eresia eunice *(Peru).*
RIGHT: *a day-flying arctiid moth,* Dysschema irene *(Brazil).*

way for mimicry of toxic insects by chemically unprotected species (Batesian mimicry: pages 142–3) and for the evolution of warning patterns in common among chemically protected species (Müllerian mimicry: see opposite).

The defensive chemicals used by insects, irrespective of whether they are home-made or of plant origin, are classifiable into two broad groups, based on the effects on predators: the so-called Class I and Class II compounds.

Class I compounds are to a greater or lesser extent poisonous and harmful. There are two sorts: those which have an immediate effect such as sudden, severe pain and irritation, such as found in the venom of wasps and bees, and those with a delayed action, which cause blistering and vomiting. The latter are based on a lizard or bird's ability to associate even delayed effects with eating a particular type of prey. Delayed-action compounds may serve as a reminder if the original foul taste is

The harlequin livery of these nymphs of a plant-bug, Pachlis sp. (Mexico), signals to would-be predators that a very nasty taste awaits the unwary.

ANT, WASP AND BEE MIMICS

Ants, wasps and bees defend themselves with a painful sting. Those ants and bees which are stingless have other chemical weapons at their disposal: a dense spray of formic acid (ants) and corrosive, blistering secretions from glands in the head (stingless bees).

It is not surprising that such chemically well-protected insects are models for a wide range of unarmed insects, as shown here. Wasp and bee mimics resemble their models in their warning coloration, usually alternating bands of black and yellow or orange. These mimics are, like their models, flower feeders and thus are often seen together with their models at flowers. Summertime thistles and hogweed flowers are good places to see hoverflies and beetles rubbing shoulders with their wasp and bee mimics.

Many wasp mimics and, especially, ant mimics resemble their models not only in colour but also in body form and gait.

RIGHT: *A convincing ant mimic, a bug,* Hyalymenus *sp. (Mexico), feeds on fruits.*

BELOW: *Several wasp-mimicking hoverflies,* Syrphus ribesii *(UK), share an* Angelica *flower with a tree wasp,* Dolichovespula sylvestris.

BELOW: *Another specialist bee mimic, the hoverfly* Eristalis tenax *(bottom) and its model, the honeybee* Apis mellifera *(UK).*

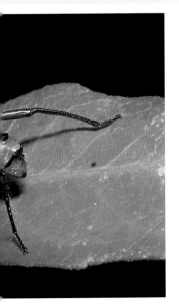

RIGHT: *A wasp-mimicking bug,* Lissocarta vespiformis, *in a Peruvian rainforest.*

BELOW: *A specialist bumblebee mimic, the hoverfly* Volucella bombylans *(right), shares a flower with its model, the bumblebee* Bombus lucorum *(UK).*

Larvae of a sawfly, Perga *sp. (Australia), rear up in unison as a threat display, emitting at the same time a foul-tasting secretion.*

relived during vomiting. Delayed-action effects thus reinforce the immediate effects of the noxious compounds.

Class II compounds are, by themselves, harmless. They may simply deter a predator. Some Class II compounds are evocative scents and have a reinforcing effect; they become associated in the predator's memory with the more violent effects of the Class I compounds.

The chemical protection enjoyed by many insects does not, however, make them invincible. In the escalation and counter-escalation of predator–prey relations, some insectivorous birds have evolved the ability to cope with whatever weapons their prey can mobilize.

Bee-eaters can disarm a wasp or bee by deftly removing the sting in a split second. And monarch butterflies, *Danaus plexippus*, roosting at their wintering sites in Mexico (see Chapter 3), are sometimes eaten by black-headed grosbeaks, which seem to be totally immune to the poisons stored in the butterflies' tissues.

Another bird, the black-headed oriole, is not completely immune to the monarch's poisons, but has the ability to detect variations in the amount of poison present in different individuals. It selects those monarchs that are less toxic than usual.

Lubber grasshoppers, *Romalea* spp., are particularly well protected. They are large and warningly coloured, and enhance their warning patterns by living gregariously. Their chemical weapon takes the form of a highly toxic, pungent-smelling and volatile spray, together with a loud hissing noise, which deters all lizards and birds – except, that is, for one species. The loggerhead shrike is not put off. It catches the lubbers and, very quickly, impales them on thorns, leaving them there for some days.

The collection of impaled lubber grasshoppers serves not only as a larder but also, for male loggerhead shrikes, as a territorial and sexual signal. The message to female shrikes is this: 'Look at me, I can accumulate a mass of these toxic grasshoppers with no ill-effects, so let's make babies together.'

Even the loggerhead shrike is not immune to the emetic effects of lubbers but, by leaving the prey impaled for several days, the toxins are denatured by exposure to the sun.

Insect defence policies have evolved in an ever-escalating arms race. They have been doing this for millions of years, long before the Dr Strangeloves of our own species sought to develop ever-nastier ways of killing people.

When pecked by a hungry bird or harassed by a lizard, this grasshopper, Phymateus morbillosus *(South Africa), defends itself by exuding a foul-smelling, toxic foam.*

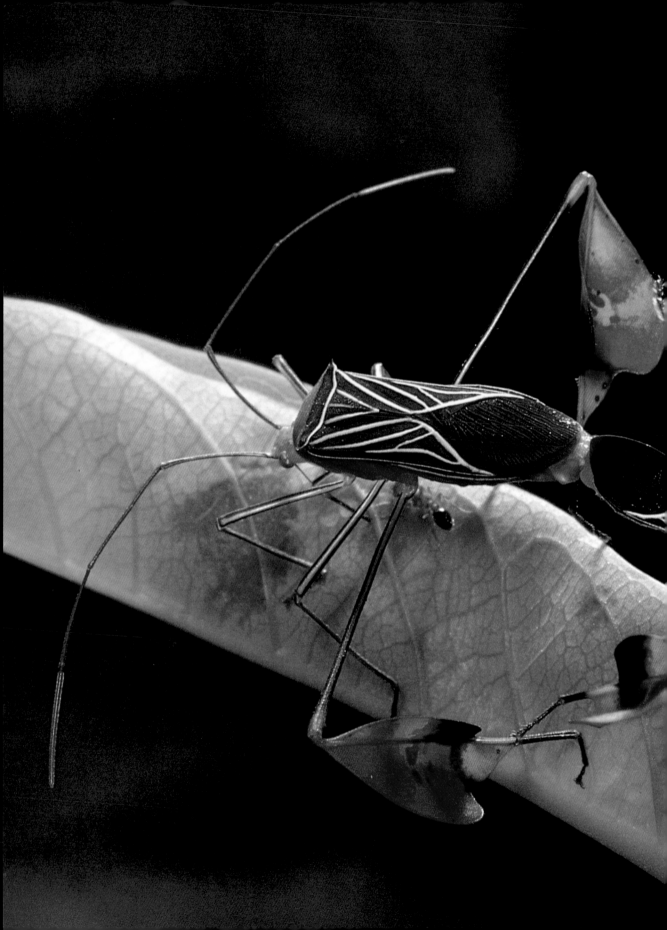

6

MAKING
MORE
INSECTS

Courtship, mating
and parental care

A mating pair of a flag-footed bug, Aniscocelis
flavolineata *(Costa Rica). Back-to-back mating
is common among true bugs.*

I F THE OFFSPRING of a pair of houseflies all survived, as did their offspring and so on, after a year they would form a sphere 93 million miles in diameter – the distance between Earth and the sun. That they *do not* do so is the result of many checks: environmental conditions, parasites, predators and disease. That flies *can* do so testifies to their enormous reproductive potential. Insects are clearly very good at making more insects; apart from dispersal, this is the main function of all adult insects, ensuring that as many copies of their genes as possible get into the next generation. And they have evolved many bizarre ways of accomplishing this.

OPPOSITE: *A mêlée of cotton-stainer bugs,* Dysdercus *sp. (Kenya), mating and feeding on a cassava plant.*

MATE RECOGNITION

Before mating, each insect has to be able to recognize the opposite sex of its own species. The sheer numbers of insects at any one locality make this an apparently daunting task: on average, there are 10 billion insects per square kilometre (14 billion per square mile). Many of these will be closely related species. For this reason, insects have evolved many intricate and elegant ways of mate recognition through a variety of different channels. According to species, these may involve specific scents, sounds, semaphore signals, pulses of flashing light or a combination of two or more of these means of communication.

BELOW: *An aggregation of male shieldbugs,* Eysarcoris fabricii *(UK), displays in the hope of attracting mates. They produce a mating call by stridulation – making a noise by rasping two body parts together.*

In many cases, the vigour and intensity of these signals give the female insect the opportunity to assess the quality of her suitors. A female can also assess a male's fitness, in the genetic sense, by the quality of a resource, such as an egg-laying site, he has won by fighting rivals. Quality assessment is most highly developed in those insects where males offer courtship gifts to females (pages 154–5).

Many closely related insect species are virtually identical in appearance except for the structure of the male genitalia. Entomologists use the genitalia of male insects as a kind of fingerprint to identify them to species. This has led to the suggestion that insects use genitalia in the same way, as a kind of calling card. In this way, the so-called 'lock-and-key' theory of insect genitalia was born and became popular.

COURTSHIP GIFTS

ABOVE: *An unnamed female bush cricket (katydid) (Brazil), eats the spermatophylax donated by the male during mating.*

BELOW: *Not above some deception, a male dancefly, Polyblepharis opaca (UK), with willow-seed fluff he wrapped in silk and used as a nuptial gift, and will try to use again.*

A recurrent theme in the sex lives of insects is the assessment of potential mates for fitness, in the sense of genetic soundness. Often, it is the females that make the assessment and the males that have to demonstrate some kind of prowess. The provision of courtship gifts is one way that the males of some species offer themselves for scrutiny.

The offering of gifts has evolved independently among scorpionflies (which are not true flies and belong to the order Mecoptera) and danceflies, which are true flies.

Males of the common European scorpionfly, *Panorpa communis*, have two principal ways of offering a gift. First, a male seeks an insect corpse as a gift – often this will be stolen from a spider's web. He then settles down next to his gift and emits a sex pheromone (sexual scent), which attracts a female. She eats the gift while the male mates with her.

If he cannot find a suitable insect corpse, he adopts another ploy. He deposits a drop of rapidly drying saliva on to a leaf and draws it out into a pillar shape. He sits by this and again calls to passing females with his pheromone. A female can assess the fitness of her potential mate by the amount of saliva offered. If she accepts him, she eats the gift while they mate.

With both corpse and saliva gifts, other rival males may be attracted and try to steal the gift, sometimes with success. The male will defend his gift by trying to fight off his rivals. They assess the size and value of the gift; the bigger it is, the longer they are prepared to fight for it.

Hangingflies are relatives of the scorpionflies, and males also offer gifts to females. They have raptorial hindlegs with which they grasp insect prey.

The behaviour of the North American species, *Bittacus apicalis*, is typical. Armed with a gift, the male flies through damp woodland, carrying his prey by his hindlegs. Periodically, he lands on a plant and hangs from it with his elongate forelegs. At the same time, he everts a pair of pheromone-emitting glands at the tip of his abdomen and calls for females.

A receptive female will engage her genitalia with those of the male and start to mate while testing the size and, hence, quality of the gift by rolling it around with her legs and probing it with her mouthparts. She

A mating pair of a hanging scorpionfly, Harpobittacus *spp. (Australia). The female is eating a fly captured previously by the male, which he offered to her as a nuptial gift.*

eats while mating and is quite capable of terminating the nuptials before sperm transfer is complete. The larger the gift, the longer she is prepared to mate, so it pays the male to find the biggest prey he can.

Danceflies, sometimes called assassin flies, are true flies, and courtship behaviour involving gifts is common and widespread among them. Typically, the males of species of *Empis* assemble in dense swarms, their bobbing flight giving them the name 'danceflies'. Males with a nuptial gift, usually a fly, are attractive to females and the latter receive the gift in return for mating. They eat it while mating proceeds. When it is finished, males very often snatch the gift away and use it again several times in subsequent matings and, with

time and usage, the gift becomes increasingly battered and decreases in food value.

Male *Empis* often attempt to steal gifts from other males. Sometimes, large species of *Empis* use smaller species as prey and some will even kill members of their own species for use as gifts. *Empis* males are not above deception and sometimes offer the useless seeds of dandelions as gifts.

The males of *Hilara* species wrap their gifts in a balloon of silk. Here, deception is common, with inedible objects such as a piece of petal or seed being gift-wrapped rather than a genuine gift of an insect. Sometimes, a male dispenses with a gift altogether and simply offers an empty balloon of silk.

At the time this theory was gaining ground, the extent of courtship rituals and the use of specific scents and sounds were not fully realized. In the light of what we know now, the lock-and-key theory seems a little naive. It implies that male insects fly around at random, inserting their genitalia into any apparently suitable female and, if his 'key' fits her 'lock', they mate. They certainly do not do this. Insects are able to filter out the billions of irrelevant individuals, the reproductive background noise, and mate with members of their own species.

This does not mean that male genitalia are not involved in mate recognition. Rather, a more realistic approach is to regard the specific distinctness of male genitalia as the last in a chain of signals and counter signals between the opposite sexes, a kind of internal courtship.

FINDING A MATE

Insects have many ways of bringing the sexes together. Some seem crude and random, others are highly sophisticated and involve great sensory finesse and the integration of much complicated behaviour. Usually, it is the males which are the active seekers after mates.

Scramble competition

To the human observer, scramble competition seems like a crude rough and tumble, a mass of random attempts at grabbing a mate. In Britain and Europe, a good place to see scramble competition in action is any clump of thistles or hogweed in high summer. Here there are masses of common soldier beetles, *Rhagonycha fulva*, milling about over the flowers, with many pairs in copulation, the females walking around, grazing on pollen grains and carrying the males on their backs. There is a constant jostling between males for access to females. There is apparently no courtship and no finesse involved here, but scent may well play a role initially in bringing the sexes together.

Scramble competition is also seen in mayflies, where both sexes swarm in vast numbers for a very short period. Almost immediately after mating, the male dies and the female returns to water, where her body more or less explodes, releasing her eggs.

Among males of the solitary bee, *Colletes cunicularius*, competition for access to females is literally a scramble. This species nests in sandy heaths and coastal dunes. Males emerge a few days before females and

OPPOSITE: *Many insects seek mates at flowers. Here, several mating pairs of the soldier beetle,* Rhagonycha fulva *(UK), consort on flowers of hogweed.*

JOUSTING MALES

We are used to the idea of male mammals jousting for access to nubile females: in spring, alpine valleys in Central Europe ring to the sound of head-butting chamois goats. But male contests of this sort are found among insects, too.

As with the chamois and rutting red deer, male insects which indulge in jousting contests may have antlers (some flies), eyestalks (some flies), large snouts (brenthid weevils) or jaws that are massively developed (stag beetles).

The males of stalk-eyed flies compete for control of a resource of interest to egg-laying females. As their name implies, their eyes are mounted at the ends of long stalks. Competing males stand head to head, eyestalk to eyestalk and, in this way, can accurately assess each other's size because head width is a function of overall body size and fighting prowess. This

assessment enables the smaller of a competing pair to depart and avoid a damaging fight. Similar assessments may also take place initially between horned and massively jawed beetles.

When two competing beetles are more evenly matched in size, then a trial-of-strength contest ensues. Stag beetles and large, tropical horned beetles are typical: the males fight for control of a particular territory or resource, in this case a log in which females will come to lay their eggs. They use their jaws or horns to wrestle their opponent off the log.

The winner of a trial-of-strength contest assumes control of the log and mates with any females which come to lay eggs. The visiting female can be assured that she is mating with a male that has proved his strength and, therefore, his genetic soundness, by winning a fight or series of fights with rival males.

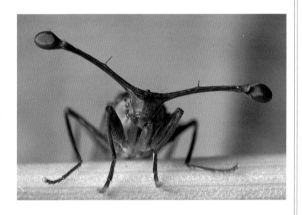

LEFT: *Betting on the outcome of contesting male rhinoceros beetles (Chiang Mai, Thailand). Males of these beetles fight to gain control of prominent logs. Log-owners have easier access to females for mating.*

RIGHT: *This male stag beetle,* Lucanus cervus *(UK), sports gigantic jaws which are useless for eating. Instead, males of this and other species of stag beetles use their jaws in trial-of-strength contests to establish ownership of mating territories on a log.*

ABOVE: *With eyes at the end of long stalks, males of* Diopsis *sp. (South Africa) face up to each other in territorial disputes: males with shorter stalks stand down in favour of those with longer stalks.*

patrol the nest site. Soon, groups of males are attracted to particular spots on the surface of the sand and start digging frantically and jostling for position. They are digging for virgin females, which are making their way to the surface. As they do so, females give off a heavy, sweet scent called linalool and the digging males home in on this.

As soon as a female is exposed, there is tremendous excitement among the males. They fight for access to the female. Eventually, one mounts her. Mating lasts for about eight to ten minutes and, for the first half of this period, the mating pair are attractive to other males and many may cluster round, sometimes forming a fist-sized ball, which may roll down the dune. The half-way stage in mating is marked by a series of sudden, loud buzzes, and at this point the other males immediately leave and seek other females or mating pairs. The buzzing is a signal that sperm transfer has started; the competing males leave because the female mates only once and there is no longer any point in trying to displace the mating male. Up to the half-way point, though, there is still a chance that the mating male may be dislodged and, therefore, it is still worth fighting for access to the female.

The females of many solitary (non-social) wasps and bees mate only once. This means that, as time goes on, the males are confronted with a diminishing resource; for this reason, there is extreme competition between males.

Territoriality

We are familiar with the notion of male mammals, such as dogs or hyenas, having territories, which they defend and scent-mark with urine or anal gland secretions. Many male insects are territorial and scent or song may be the boundary markers.

Insects such as male dragonflies, however, do not use scent to mark their territories. Instead, they patrol constantly, relying on their acute vision to detect interloping males. In a male hawker dragonfly, such as the emperor dragonfly, *Anax imperator*, territory ownership is decided by fighting; a male may end up with exclusive rights to a single small pond. With larger bodies of water, several males may have adjoining territories. A successful territory holder has almost exclusive mating rights to any receptive females which enter. Territories may change hands over time, especially if an aging, lone male has been fighting off all comers for some time.

A courting pair of robberflies, Cyrtopogon ruficornis *(France). The male, on the right, bobs his raised abdomen in a series of semaphore signals which indicate to the female that her suitor is of the correct species.*

Sometimes, a male's territory contains a resource of value to the female. Thus males of the solitary bee *Anthidium manicatum* set up territories at clumps of flowers that the females visit for pollen and nectar. The males seem not to mark their territories with scent. Instead, they hover in and around the territory, pouncing on any rival males which enter or any other flower-visiting insects.

The tip of the male's abdomen is armed with a row of sharp spines. When in combat with, say, a worker honeybee, the male grabs the worker with his legs and stabs her with the spines. This often kills the honeybee; the territory of an aggressive male of *A. manicatum* may be littered with the bodies of dead and dying honeybees and butterflies.

The reason for all this aggression is simple. By excluding insects from the patch of flowers that forms his territory, a male can offer a potential mate a protected and rich resource, a food bonanza not only for her, but also for their offspring, whose cells she is provisioning with nectar and honey. Unusually for solitary bees, the females of this species mate more than once and, more often than not, with the territory holder. It may well be that multiple matings are the price the female is prepared to pay for access to a protected food source.

All is not entirely simple with this bee, however. The males are larger than the females, which is unusual: female solitary bees are normally the larger sex. Territory-holding males of *A. manicatum* are larger than non-territory-holders, which is what one might expect. But this does not mean that the smaller males are deprived of matings.

Smaller males have facial markings which approximate to those of females; they also fly more slowly, like females, without the rapid darting flight of territory-holders. When a small male enters a territory, the territorial male seems to regard him as a non-receptive female and largely ignores him. This sneaky male strategy, pretending to be a female, allows the smaller males to have opportunistic matings. This species is found over much of Europe, including Britain, and also in parts of the eastern United States, where it was accidentally introduced.

Male bumblebees, *Bombus* spp., have a variant of territorial behaviour, which does not involve aggression. Several males of one species may patrol a shared circuit, which has several vantage points along its length. These may be prominent shrubs, an old tree stump, a rock outcrop, etc. While flying around the circuit, each male stops regularly and deposits scent droplets at one of the vantage points or on a leaf. The scent is produced in glands in the head and is a blend of sweet-scented oils, easily detected by the human nose. Receptive, virgin females which cross the circuit near a scent-marked spot loiter until another male comes around the circuit; the several males on the circuit all fly in the same direction and thus rarely encounter one another.

Each species of bumblebee produces its own characteristic scent, and this is the medium of species recognition. In late summer, the fields and hedgerows of Britain, Europe and North America are a network of overlapping circuits patrolled by many species, but the scented calling cards ensure that mating between different species is only very rare.

Advertising

Male, and some female, insects advertise their readiness to mate in a variety of ways. Whatever the signals used, the message must be clear and unequivocal: it must identify the species of the calling individual.

Sound is a common form of communication. Male grasshoppers, bush crickets (katydids), leafhoppers, shieldbugs, cicadas, some moths and midges all produce sounds to attract the attention of females. The volume and pattern of sound pulses, the wavelengths used, are all characteristic of the species involved.

Male grasshoppers generate their songs by stridulation, rubbing a row of tiny pegs on the inner sides of the hindlegs against a specially hardened vein on the forewing. The spacing, and size, of the pegs contribute to the uniqueness of the species' song.

OVERLEAF: *A courting pair of crickets,* Nisitrus *spp. (Borneo). The male, on the left, sings by rubbing together specialized areas at the bases of the wings; he uses his raised wing cases as amplifiers as he sings to his intended mate.*

Bush crickets and true crickets make their song by rubbing together two specialized areas at the base of the wings. Many species use their raised wings to act as resonators, and some construct special mud sound boxes which considerably amplify the song.

The song of certain male cicadas is the loudest of all animal noises. These bugs have a remarkable structure for generating sound, the tymbal, one at each side of the base of the abdomen. The tymbals are a special click mechanism under muscular control; they click back and forth at more than 4–7000Hz, the clicks fusing together to make a deafening whine which in some species reaches 112 decibels. Abdominal air sacs resonate sympathetically with the tymbals and act as super amplifiers. Each species has its characteristic song.

Cicadas are superb ventriloquists. This makes it impossible for the vertebrate ear to locate the position of a calling male. Thus, while a male cicada is broadcasting his presence loud and clear, predators cannot locate his exact position. Only a receptive female, ready and willing to mate, can locate him.

Other bugs, such as planthoppers, have tymbals, but their song is transmitted as vibrations through leaves and green plant stems.

It is well known that whales, dolphins and porpoises communicate by songs, water being an ideal medium for conducting low-frequency sounds over great distances. Male water boatmen, *Notonecta* spp., make sounds by rubbing together roughened areas of their forelegs. They can generate 40 decibels, which carries under water a distance of 40m (131ft). A receptive female calls back with a song of her own and the male homes in on her. When he makes contact, he performs a loud courtship song which often stimulates nearby males to rowdy singing of their own, and outbreaks of fighting between them.

Meanwhile, the successful male produces a shrill call as he mounts the female and they descend to the bottom of the pond, where she hangs on to the bottom with her legs. Copulation is only successful if she continues to do this. Thereafter, she is unattractive to other males.

Advertising for a mate by singing is not without its risks. Apart from alerting predatory birds, there are more sinister implications. For example, the songs of the North American cricket, *Gryllus integer*, have been hijacked by a parasitic tachinid fly, which has evolved the ability to recognize the song and home in on it. The female fly lays her eggs on the cricket and these produce larvae which bore into his body and

OPPOSITE: *A male cicada,* Henicopsaltria eydouxi *(Australia), sings on a eucalyptus tree to attract a mate. Cicada songs are the loudest of all insect calls, frequently achieving 112 decibels.*

consume his tissues. For a male cricket, the urge to make a genetic investment in the next generation is so strong that the risk of attracting the parasitic fly is an acceptable cost: there is a good statistical chance that by the time his songs have attracted the fly, he will have had at least one successful mating.

For many insects, advertising for a mate means emitting an attractive scent or sex pheromone. A pheromone is a scent which is emitted by one individual animal and which affects the behaviour of another of the same species. Pheromones are widespread in the animal kingdom, including our own species. But the virtuosos of pheromones are the insects, and none more so than the moths.

In moths, it is usually the female which is the calling sex. And since the 1950s, the sex pheromones of several hundred moth species have been identified chemically by scientists.

Many moths produce very similar mixtures of volatile compounds as sex pheromones. The particular blend produced by a species, in terms of constituent chemicals and their relative proportions, imparts the species-specific nature of the pheromone. Thus, the females of several species may be calling simultaneously at one locality, but each is transmitting a unique signature of scents that only the males of the correct species can detect.

And, as we have seen in Chapter 2, male moths are particularly well equipped in terms of ultrasensitive antennae (see also diagram right). Male emperor moths, *Saturnia pavonia*, can detect a calling female over a distance of 11km (6.8 miles), which is truly impressive when one considers the dilution which must occur over this kind of distance.

The information transmitted by an insect's sex pheromone is not just the specific identity of the caller; it also transmits information about the quality of the male relative to rivals. The fact that pheromones tend to be more or less complex blends increases the potential for this kind of information to be transmitted. Although moths and butterflies have been the best studied groups as far as communication by scent is concerned, sex pheromones are very widespread in the insects and may be universal.

Self-generated light is another channel of sexual communication. In North America, there are beetles which generate flashing lights for sexual communication. The males of these fireflies, *Photinus* spp., emit pulses of light, the frequency and duration of which are unique to the

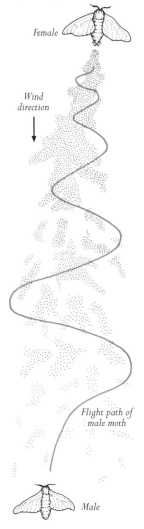

BELOW: *A female moth emits a sex pheromone, which flows downwind in an ever-diluting plume of vapour. A male detects this and flies in a zig-zag path up the concentration gradient of pheromone until he finds the female.*

Female

Wind direction

Flight path of male moth

Male

OPPOSITE: *Female termites, Odontotermes spp. (Nepal), calling males by releasing a sexual scent or pheromone, which they disperse by flapping their wings.*

ABOVE: *A male red-tipped clearwing moth,* Dipsosphecia scopigera *(UK), sends out his calling card, a sex pheromone from glands in the tip of his abdomen.*

OPPOSITE: *Many male insects are smaller than their females, as in this mating pair of grasshoppers,* Chrysochraon dispar *(Germany).*

species; the females of each species answer in their own characteristic pattern. In this way, the sexes find each other and mate.

As with the calling males of the cricket *Gryllus integer*, advertising in this way carries some risk. The females of another group of fireflies, *Photuris* spp., mimic the reply patterns of female *Photinus* and thus lure *Photinus* males, which they eat. Each of these *femme fatale* species can mimic the reply patterns of up to five species of *Photinus*.

Another way to attract mates is for males to assemble in large numbers in a special kind of display or lek. This is well known for some birds and mammals but more and more instances are being found among insects. A lek is a conspicuous aggregation of males which stages some kind of display at a vantage point such as a prominent shrub or rock outcrop. Typically, a lek takes place at a site which has no resources of interest to females other than a large number of males. The females thus have a free choice from among many competing males, which might compete for the best positions within the lek.

In Britain and Europe, males of the mining bee, *Lasioglossum calceatum*, stage leks on the dead flowerheads of knapweed. Thirty or forty assemble and spend their time wheeling around with erect antennae; they shiver their semi-iridescent wings. This display, possibly combined with a scent, attracts females, which hover around the dead flowerhead. Every now and then, one of the females darts into the mass of males and selects a mate.

In the American salt marsh moth, *Estigmene acrea*, lek behaviour is one of two mating strategies. Females of this moth emit a pheromone and males fly upwind towards them and copulate without any courtship. Alternatively, males assemble and form a lek on vegetation. Lekking males evert their abdominal coremata, large, paired tubular and branched structures filled with a greenish liquid. Almost certainly, the males emit a pheromone and females are attracted to the lek, select a male and mate immediately; males are also attracted to the lek, which gradually increases in size.

MATING AND
SPERM COMPETITION

When two insects mate, the male transfers sperm to a special storage sac in the female, the spermatheca. When the female lays her eggs, each passes the entrance to the spermatheca; the female releases a little amount of seminal fluid as each egg passes and thus fertilizes it.

The anatomical facts of this pose problems for the males of species which mate more than once. On average, the sperm released at any one time by a female is that from the most recent mating. Sperm release is therefore, generally, on a 'last in, first out' basis. Sperm precedence, as this is called, is a problem for the male: he may have invested considerable time and energy in finding and courting a female, and yet a more recent male's sperm gets to fertilize his mate's eggs. Ensuring paternity is therefore a real problem, but many male insects have evolved ways of minimizing this loss.

Mate guarding is the simplest way of doing this: a male remains with his mate for a long time after mating until she has laid her eggs. This is common in many beetles and bugs. Male dragonflies and damselflies have some very ingenious ways of overcoming sperm precedence. Some dragonflies have inflatable lobes at the tip of the penis. During mating, but before ejaculation, the lobes inflate and compress the sperm from previous matings deeper into the female's spermatheca. This ensures that there is a greater chance that it will be his sperm rather than a rival's which will fertilize the next batch of eggs to be laid.

LEFT: *A mating pair of the leaf-beetle,* Doryphora testudo *(Peru). Expanded suction pads on the feet of the male enable him to grasp his mate firmly.*

Some dragonflies and damselflies have highly modified tips to the penis, which actually scrape out any sperm from previous matings from the female's spermatheca.

Other ploys used by male insects to overcome the problem of sperm precedence involve making the female unattractive to subsequent males. Thus, the males of many mosquitoes produce a scent in their seminal fluid, matrone, which renders his mate unattractive to other males; just to underline the point, he also secretes a jelly-like mating plug with which he blocks up the female's genital opening, so that she cannot mate again until she has cleared the blockage by laying eggs which will be fertilized by the plug-maker's sperm. Once again, insects got there before us: they even invented the chastity belt.

The males of some butterflies achieve a similar effect by depositing an anti-aphrodisiac scent on their mates: they have invented the chemical chastity belt.

If sperm precedence is a problem to be overcome by many male insects, there is one group of bug species in which the males turn this to their own advantage. Males of the species of *Xylocoris* will attempt to mate with any females they encounter. They also increase their chances of paternity by homosexual rape. A male will pounce on another male and mate with him, ejaculating sperm into the other male's reproductive tract. On the principle of last in, first out, when the rape victim next mates it will be the rapist's sperm, not his own, which will be deposited in the female; the rapist has therefore mated by proxy.

OPPOSITE: *A female variable longhorn beetle,* Sternotomis variabilis *(Kenya), lays her eggs in wood, guarded by her mate. By guarding her, he protects his genetic investment in the eggs she lays; he also prevents other males mating with her and thus avoids sperm competition.*

WHEELS AND TANDEMS

The males of dragonflies and damselflies have two sets of genitalia each. One is in the normal place, at the tip of the abdomen; this is really just a simple opening for the release of sperm. The other, secondary genitalia, are at the base of the abdomen, on the underside of the second segment.

Before mating, a male transfers sperm from the opening at the tip of the abdomen to the secondary

LEFT: *A pair of ruddy darter dragonflies,* Sympetrum sanguineum *(UK), in tandem flight prior to mating; the male clasps the female at the back of her head.*

BELOW: *The pair now adopt the wheel position for mating. Later, they will fly in tandem while the female lays her eggs.*

genitalia. This requires considerable flexibility on his part. The reason why males are doubly endowed and so abdominally flexible is to free the pair of claspers at the end of the abdomen, to be used in grasping the female.

After finding a receptive female, the male uses his claspers to grasp the female by the top of her head. They then fly together for some time in this tandem position. Eventually, they land on a plant or branch and assume the so-called wheel position. This involves the female, still in the grip of the male's claspers, bending her abdomen forward so that her genitalia engage with the secondary genitalia and sperm transfer takes place. This may take ten to fifteen minutes.

After this wheel position, the pair fly off again in tandem. In many species, the male assists the female in egg-laying by hovering with her in tandem while she drops her eggs into the water of a pond, lake or river. Male damselflies also assist their mates in the same way as they lay eggs into the tissues of water plants. Female damselflies are equipped with a blade-like ovipositor for making an incision in the plant to receive the egg.

The penis of the secondary genitalia of male damselflies has a special, spoon-shaped structure for scooping out any sperm which might have been deposited by another male in a previous mating. This is a way that the male can ensure that it is his sperm, not a rival's, that fertilizes the next batch of eggs to be laid. In this way, he ensures his paternity. Devices of this sort are increasingly being found in insects where sperm precedence prevails (see pages 169–71).

Male-assisted egg-laying: a pair of the azure damselfly, Coenagrion puella *(UK), in tandem flight, the male holding the female while she lays eggs into water weeds.*

PARENTAL CARE

Parental care is almost entirely restricted to female insects, but males of the assassin bug, Rhinocoris tristis (Kenya), are exceptional. This one guards his mate's egg clutch, chasing away the tiny wasps, egg parasites, trying to lay their eggs into his offspring.

After all the effort and energy expended by insects in finding a mate, the offspring, especially in the growing nymphal or larval stages, may be very vulnerable to predators, parasites and the vagaries of climate. Many insects therefore protect their genetic investment by some form of parental care. By doing this, they increase the chances that at least some of their offspring will survive long enough to be parents in their own right. Such is the tyranny of the genes.

The simplest form of parental care is for the females to lay their eggs

in or on the larval food, such being the case with butterflies, moths, beetles and many flies.

More active parental care involves the mother remaining with the eggs until they hatch out and can fend for themselves. This is the case with the so-called parent shieldbug, *Elasmucha grisea*, which remains with her egg batch on a birch leaf until they hatch. She protects them against predatory insects and

MATERNAL CARE IN A FUNGUS BEETLE

The tropical fungus beetle, *Pselaphicus giganteus*, inhabits Central American forests and some Caribbean islands. Unlike most beetles, the females of this species show a simple form of social behaviour: a mother remains with her young to ensure their safety and well-being.

A female *Pselaphicus giganteus* lays her eggs on a fallen log. She remains with them, guarding them from danger. She is herself warningly coloured, suggesting that she is poisonous or, at least, highly distasteful.

When the eggs hatch into larvae, she shepherds them to their first fungus meal. The larvae apparently feed only on a single species of fungus, *Polyporus tenuiculus*. Feeding is so rapid and intense that defecation is a continuous process. When they have eaten their fill on one fungus, the female guides the larvae to another. As she does so, she drags the tip of her abdomen along the

log surface, with rapid, side-to-side wiping movements. This is highly suggestive that she is laying a scent trail for her larvae to follow.

She is a most attentive mother, constantly fussing around her band of larvae, touching them with her antennae and running about to round up stragglers. The larval stage lasts only four days before pupation. All the time, the mother is in attendance.

Maternal care in this beetle may have evolved as a result of the extremely specialized diet of the larvae. The fungus is very short-lived, lasting only three to four days. It is also sporadically distributed, so by staying with her juvenile offspring, directing them to sources of food and guarding them, a female *Pselaphicus giganteus* maximizes their survival and thus maximizes the return on her genetic investment.

the tiny wasps, *Trichogramma* spp., which lay eggs in those of other insects. Parenting of this kind is common also in other shieldbugs, and a Peruvian leaf beetle, *Omaspides* sp., does the same. An African praying mantis, *Tarachodula pantherina*, sits on top of her egg pod until the nymphs hatch.

In terms of egg-guarding, it is the females which are most often involved, though paternal care is known from some insects. The females of belostomatid water bugs lay their eggs on the backs of their mates. The males carry them around until they hatch. More active egg-guarding is seen in males of an African assassin bug, *Rhinocoris tristis*, which remain with the egg batch and chase away any wasps trying to parasitize it.

The myriad ways which insects have evolved to make more insects is truly amazing, and many more strategies of mating, courtship and parental care undoubtedly remain to be discovered. All testify to one of the most extreme pressures of being alive: ensuring that genes span the generations.

LEFT: *A female fungus beetle,* Pselaphicus giganteus *(Trinidad), gathers together her brood of tiny larvae to lead them to a new fungus on which to feed.*

ABOVE: *A female parent shieldbug,* Elasmucha grisea *(UK), guards her nymphs while they feed, protecting them from predatory insects. She has already been successful in protecting the egg stage from egg-parasitizing wasps.*

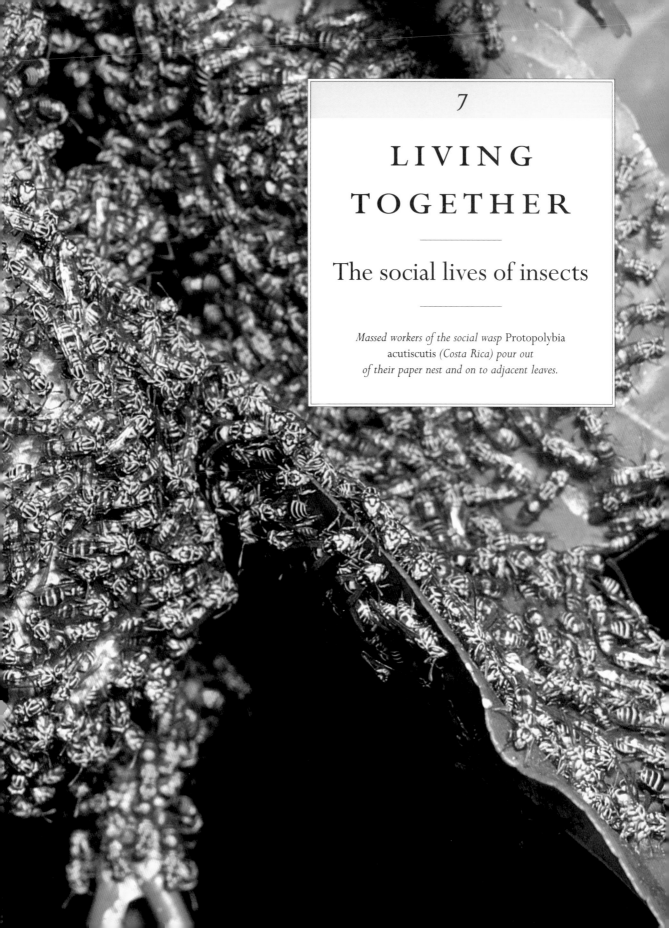

7

LIVING
TOGETHER

The social lives of insects

Massed workers of the social wasp Protopolybia
acutiscutis *(Costa Rica) pour out
of their paper nest and on to adjacent leaves.*

OMPLEX SOCIETIES developed among insects as well as ourselves. Like human society, insects have large workforces, with specialist castes: there is a division of labour which depends on co-operation between individuals.

Fortunately for us, the similarity ends here. Insect societies work on very different principles to ours: usually only one or a few individuals, the queens, have the opportunity to breed. And they are fed and their offspring nurtured by workers that themselves never reproduce and many of which will sacrifice their lives in defence of queen and colony. An insect society is thus rigidly organized; there is no room for individuality, and its workings have been likened to a super-organism.

THE KINDS OF SOCIAL BEHAVIOUR

Not all kinds of social interactions between insects are so complex and highly organized. There are many levels of social behaviour; the simplest is based on a relationship between mother and offspring which is prolonged beyond the normal pattern for insects, which is to lay eggs in a suitable place and move on.

Subsocial behaviour

We saw in Chapter 6 how some insects increase their own reproductive success by guarding their young during the vulnerable early stages. This is the subsocial level of social development and is now known from at least seventeen families of beetles. Almost all of them are associated with rich but scattered food sources which are short-lived, such as dead wood, fungi, dung and carrion.

Some beetles have taken things a little further than the species we saw in Chapter 6. In Japan, females of the tiny rove beetle, *Oxyporus japonicus*, excavate nest chambers in the young stems of toadstools. The female lays her clutch of eggs in this and then remains with them until they have safely hatched into larvae. She protects them from other intruding females of the same species and other predatory beetles. If mothers are removed experimentally, the eggs are eaten by other females, sometimes within five minutes of the removal of the mother.

Burying beetles make good parents. Both larvae and adults of *Necrophorus* spp. feed on carrion. The adults can detect a rotting corpse from some distance.

Usually, a *Necrophorus* defends its carcass against members of the same sex, but a single mated pair co-operate in burying the corpse. In some species, four or five females may collaborate and can bury, say, a dead mouse more quickly than one beetle working alone. In this situation, one female becomes dominant and she lays her eggs on the buried mouse.

She feeds her larvae by regurgitating a rich liquid of predigested mouse, which she feeds directly to her larvae in turn. She signals meal times by rasping her abdomen against her wing cases.

Burying beetles can detect corpses which have been buried. They will kill any young larvae they find there and lay their own eggs. For this reason, it pays parents to remain with their young larvae and protect them, and this is what some species of burying beetle do. But things are not always cosy between parents and offspring. The beetles constantly monitor the amount of food left and, if there is not enough to support

A female of the subsocial Cape Mountain cockroach, Aptera cingulata *(South Africa), with ten nymphs. Females of this unusual species give birth to live young and remain with their offspring until they can fend for themselves.*

1 8 0 · LIVING TOGETHER

all of the larvae, they kill the excess. This infanticide ensures that at least some of the survivors will live long enough to reach adulthood and reproduce themselves.

Parental care of the subsocial kind is also well developed in some cockroaches. The rhinoceros cockroach of Australia, *Macropanesthia rhinoceros*, the world's largest species, prepares a deep burrow for her offspring. Here, they remain for up to six months, feeding on material brought back by their mother's nocturnal foraging trips.

Longer-term social contact is maintained by the woodroach, *Crypto-cerus punctulatus*, found in the damp woodlands of the Appalachian mountains of eastern North America and parts of the western United States. They live in decaying wood; each colony comprises two long-lived, mated parents and 15 to 20 nymphs. The colonies live in cavities hollowed out in dead wood. And dead wood is the rather un-nutritious and almost indigestible food of these roaches.

The roaches cannot digest this for themselves and rely on symbiotic

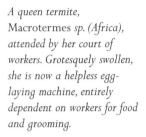

A queen termite, Macrotermes sp. (Africa), attended by her court of workers. Grotesquely swollen, she is now a helpless egg-laying machine, entirely dependent on workers for food and grooming.

protozoa which live in their hindguts. Apart from protecting the brood, parental care involves maintenance of the nest tunnels. The nymphs feed on hindgut fluids presented by the parents and, in this way, receive their own protozoa. Because the hindgut is shed at each moult, and the nymphs eat their cast skin, they re-ingest the protozoa.

The combination of gut symbionts for the digestion of cellulose with parental care is reminiscent of the situation in termites. For this reason, *Cryptocerus punctulatus* was thought, until recently, to be closely related to the ancestors of termites, but is now thought to be only a distant relation. Nevertheless, termites are clearly descended from some cockroaches and have been called the social roaches.

All termites are highly social, as are the ants. This means that we must look elsewhere for types of social behaviour which are intermediate, in an evolutionary sense, between the solitary and highly social lives of ants, termites and honeybees. And it is to bees, where sociality has evolved at least eight times, that we must look for these stages.

SOCIAL BEES

Among bees there are stages which seem to pre-date even the subsocial level of social contact. The truly solitary species never have any contact with their offspring, but nevertheless provide them with a nest and all the food they need (see pages 182–3). Beyond this level of parental care *in absentia*, there are five different levels of social behaviour: communal, quasisocial, semisocial, subsocial and eusocial bees. The first three categories all involve females of the same generation, while the last two also include overlapping generations.

Communal bees

A communal society involves several females sharing a communal nest entrance, but each has her own group of cells within the nest, usually on a side branch of the main tunnel. This is reminiscent of a human apartment block.

There is no co-operation between individuals. With the exception of the communal nest areas, all females behave as solitary bees, excavating and provisioning one cell at a time. Thus, an important and diagnostic feature of communal nests is that the number of incomplete cells equals the number of females.

SOLITARY ORIGINS

The vast majority of wasps and bees are solitary. That is, each nest is the work of a single female, working alone: there is no caste of co-operating, sterile females (workers). Social wasps and bees are in the minority and evolved from solitary species.

The typical solitary wasp or bee has an annual life-cycle. Males and females which were the offspring of the previous season emerge from their natal cells and mate. The females of most species mate only once and then go on to make a nest.

The nest is a protected site in which the mother wasp or bee constructs or excavates a succession of cells. In each cell, she stores food. In the case of wasps, this is from 1 to 20 items of insect prey she paralyses with venom from her sting.

Female bees store a mixture of nectar and pollen, which may be runny or pasty in texture, depending on their species; some bees also collect plant oils.

The is a great diversity of nest architecture. Very many species excavate nests in the soil, especially light, sandy soils, but others prefer to nest in clays. Typically, a ground nest comprises a tunnel, with one or more cells at the ends of side branches.

Most bee species line their nest cells with a waterproof, fungus-resistant secretion from a large gland in the abdomen. One family of bees, which includes the mason bees, *Osmia*, *Hoplitis* and *Chalicodoma* spp., do not produce a cell lining of their own; instead, they collect building materials from outside the nest. Many mason bees use mud or a mastic of chewed leaves and others use resin collected from sticky leaf buds or plant wounds. Leafcutter bees, *Megachile* spp., have special scissor-like jaws with which they cut pieces of leaf for use as a cell-lining material.

According to species, mason bees and leafcutter bees nest in ready-made cavities, such as beetle borings in dead wood, snail shells or holes in stones; others, such as the one shown here, make exposed nests on rocks or tree trunks. And a few nest in the ground.

When the female wasp or bee has finished provisioning her cell, she lays a single egg either on the food or on the side of the cell. She then seals the cell with a plug of soil, or the building material characteristic of her species. After a series of such cells, she may start another nest.

Female solitary wasps and bees never live to see their offspring. Their larvae feed on the stored food and then pupate and emerge the following season to restart the cycle.

The habit of sealing up one egg with all the food necessary for larval development is called mass provisioning. By contrast, social wasps and bees practise progressive feeding, that is, the larva is fed on a regular basis throughout its period of growth.

LEFT: *A tool-using wasp: this female solitary hunting wasp,* Ammophila aberti *(Utah, USA), having stocked her nest in the ground with paralysed caterpillars as food for her offspring, uses an earth pellet as a tamping tool to compact the nest closure of soil.*

RIGHT: *A solitary wasp,* Delta dimidiatipenne *(Israel), adds mud to the third of a cluster of cells on a stone. She lays a single egg in each cell after provisioning it with paralysed caterpillars.*

Some species of solitary hunting wasp do practise progressive feeding, such as the fly-hunting *Bembix texana* of North America. Another North American wasp adds a further complexity to her life. Females of the caterpillar hunting wasp, *Ammophila azteca*, are not only progressive feeders, but maintain several different nests at the same time, all in different stages of development. This requires not only an excellent memory, but the ability to divert activities from one nest to another in order to meet their individual needs. One can only marvel at the integrating and processing powers of this wasp, with a brain not much larger than a pinhead.

Whatever the details of the nesting cycle of solitary wasps and bees, all have taken one step further than the parenting insects mentioned in the last chapter: they not only construct a safe haven, a nest, for their offspring, they provide all their food. By doing this, they increase the survival chance of their offspring and the likelihood that they will themselves reproduce.

Cuckoos

Many species of solitary wasps and bees have given up building and provisioning nests for their offspring: they have become cuckoos, just like the birds of the same name. The females of cuckoo bees have lost the specialized pollen-transporting hairs on the hindlegs or undersides of the abdomen. Each cuckoo species has its own special host species, or group of closely related species.

Cuckoos have a number of adaptations for their parasitic lifestyle. The females, freed from the energy costs of nest building and provisioning, can afford to devote more of their energies to making eggs: their ovaries have at least twice as many eggs as their hosts'. And species of *Coelioxys*, the special cuckoos of leafcutter bees, *Megachile* spp., have a special blade-like modification at the tip of the abdomen with which they make an incision in the leaf lining of the host's cell and into which they lay an egg.

Perhaps the neatest adaptation for the cuckoo lifestyle is found in the males of species of *Nomada*, which develop principally in the nests of the ground-nesting bees of the genus *Andrena*. The males emerge before the females and search for nest sites of the host, where they loiter near the entrances, in between bouts of feeding at flowers. They produce a scent which is very similar to that of the host females. This attracts their own females to the area because the females home in on the scents of the host. Thus, by adding their own contribution to the overall scent signature of the host's nest site, the male *Nomada* not only attracts potential mates, he also makes it easier for the females to find hosts.

RIGHT: *Many mason bees also build exposed nests of mud. Here a female* Chalicodoma siculum *(Israel) puts a final mud seal to a cell. She has provisioned this with a mix of pollen and nectar upon which she has laid a single egg.*

Quasisocial bees

Quasisocial bees differ from communal bees in that, at any one time, the number of females is greater than the number of open, incomplete cells. This implies that there is co-operation between individuals, and the stereotyped sequences of behaviour shown by solitary bees have become more flexible. Thus, instead of a female performing the usual tasks in the same sequence (cell construction, foraging, egg-laying, cell closure), with the completion of one task being the stimulus for the next one, a quasisocial bee performs a particular task when she comes across a cell that requires a particular job. In other words, the needs of that particular cell stimulate the appropriate response in the female.

Only one egg is laid per cell, so who gets to be the egg-layer? It does not matter to a female if she works on a cell but does not get to lay an egg in it. She can be 'sure' that when she *does* find a completely provisioned cell and lays an egg in it, she will not have done all the work towards the completion of *that* cell. This case of 'you scratch my back and I'll scratch yours' has been termed 'delayed, reciprocal altruism'.

An advantage of being quasisocial may be that the constant coming and going of bees at the nest entrance deters would-be nest parasites.

Semisocial bees

These differ from the other categories in that not all the individuals of a colony are mated and have functioning ovaries. There is an incipient worker caste, but this is fluid. It seems that an individual may function as a worker for some time and then get to mate and lay some eggs.

Subsocial bees

With subsocial bees, we are on more familiar ground: they are reminiscent of the subsocial beetles and cockroaches mentioned earlier. The important evolutionary advance is that the association is between at least two different generations; a female founds a nest, rears offspring and survives long enough to associate with them as adults. Some remain in the nest and help her rear other offspring; other females leave to found their own nests. This kind of organization is found in some of the giant carpenter bees of the tropics, *Xylocopa* spp., and the dwarf carpenter bees, *Ceratina*, *Allodape* and related genera.

The overlap of generations in these subsocial bees leads us to the more highly complex societies of the eusocial bees.

Euscocial bees

Typically, a primitively eusocial nest is founded by a single, egg-laying female. Bees with this level of social behaviour include the sweat bees, *Halictus* and *Lasioglossum* spp., some orchid bees, *Eulaema* spp., and the more familiar bumblebees, *Bombus* spp.

The queen emerges from hibernation in spring and produces two or more generations of adult females which behave as workers, being involved in nest extension, foraging, brood care and nest guarding. The queen exerts dominance over her daughters by aggression and this keeps their ovaries non-functional. Towards the end of the season, the colony may be too populous for the queen's aggression to be entirely successful and some workers begin to lay eggs. Being unfertilized, they produce males. It may be that most males of sweat bees and bumblebees are produced in this way.

Eventually, a generation of males and females is produced, which leave the nest and mate. The males soon die, but the newly mated females, the next season's queens, spend some time feeding to build up their fat bodies ready for hibernation.

Because they are founded by single females, these primitively eu-social bees pass through a solitary and then subsocial phase before reaching their final, eusocial level of organization. They are best called

A worker buff-tailed bumblebee, Bombus terrestris *(UK), drinks nectar from a mallow flower,* Malva silvestris.

temporarily eusocial bees, to distinguish them from the most permanently eusocial and perennial colonies of the stingless bees of the tropics, *Melipona* and *Trigona* spp., and the seven species of honeybee, *Apis*.

The bumblebee life-cycle is matched by those of the common social wasps (yellow-jackets) and hornets, *Vespula*, *Dolichovespula* and *Vespa*. There is one major difference, though. Here, the queens do not exert dominance by aggression. Instead, they produce a pheromone, queen substance, which exerts chemical suppression of the workers' ovaries.

Honeybees: highly eusocial bees

The most sophisticated of all insect societies are those of the seven species of honeybee. The common honeybee or hive bee, *Apis mellifera*, is the species most commonly kept by beekeepers in artificial nests called hives. Honeybees have been kept in this way for at least 3000 years.

The natural distribution of *A. mellifera* was Europe, the Middle East and Africa, with a number of geographic races. It has been transported by people to all parts of the world, and now Mexico, the United States, Australia and New Zealand are the major producers of honey.

The natural nest site of the honeybee is a hollow tree or a deep rock cleft. A healthy colony consists of a single egg-laying queen and up to 80 000 workers. The workers build honeycomb in the form of double-sided wax sheets suspended vertically from the roof of the nest cavity. Each side of the comb is drawn out into hexagonal cells in which brood is reared and honey and pollen are stored.

The bees secrete the wax themselves from glands in the abdomen. They also collect resins from sticky buds and tree wounds, which they mix with pollen and a little honey to make propolis. This additional building substance is used to close gaps in hives and to narrow the nest entrance in natural nests.

As with the social wasps, the queen exerts chemical dominance over her workers with queen substance, in this case, *trans*-9-keto-2-decenoic acid. She secretes this from glands in the head. Because the queen is always attended by a court of workers which constantly groom her by licking, queen substance gets passed throughout the colony.

The tasks performed by worker honeybees are age-related. A newly emerged worker spends her first three days as a cleaner. From about days 3 to 10, she is a nurse. Glands in her head become active and enlarged and these secrete royal jelly, sometimes called bee milk. She

A worker honeybee, Apis mellifera *(UK), with nearly full pollen baskets, drinks nectar at a flower of quince,* Cydonia oblonga.

feeds this to the larvae. Those destined to be workers receive this for only three days, while those destined to become queens are fed exclusively on this rich food. It comprises a mixture of vitamins, proteins, sugars, DNA, RNA and the fatty acid *trans*-10-hydroxydecenoic acid.

At day 10, the glands which produce royal jelly atrophy and, at the same time, the wax glands in her abdomen become active: she makes the transition from nurse to worker and makes honeycomb until about day 16. For the next four days she receives pollen and nectar loads from returning foragers and places them in the comb. She ripens the nectar into the concentrate we call honey. She does this by sitting in a quiet corner of the nest, with the drop of nectar between her jaws. By constantly opening and closing her jaws, water evaporates; the nectar becomes thicker in texture and the concentration of sugar increases.

From about day 20, she is a guard at the nest entrance, and it is during this four-day period that she may be called upon to make the ultimate sacrifice. The sting of a honeybee is armed with backwardly directed barbs, which catch in the skin fibres of a mammalian or bird predator. In her struggles to get free, the bee disembowels herself, leaving the sting embedded in the skin of the enemy. She dies, but the muscles of the venom gland reservoir continue to pump venom into the wound. Another gland left with the sting emits an alarm pheromone, which recruits more workers to the attack. In this way, a mass stinging event may occur.

A thriving colony may produce 18–45kg (40–100lb) of honey per year. This is a vital resource, which keeps the colony going through winter or the dry season, when there is little or no flowering. Honey is energy-rich, and the fuel economy of bees would be the envy of car designers: a honeybee turns in an impressive 700km/cc of nectar, equivalent to 2 million mpg.

WHY BE SOCIAL?

Colony defence in social ants, wasps and bees often results in the death of defending workers. They do not reproduce, but spend all their time looking after the offspring of others. Is this altruism gone mad? Can there be a pay-off for the workers?

If the apparent devotion to slavish duty and self-sacrifice was an inspiration to moralists and despots, it was an embarrassment to Charles Darwin. With his typical candour, he pointed out that his theory of evolution by natural selection might seriously be undermined by the facts of social life among ants, wasps and bees. How can genes for such self-sacrifice survive and pass into the next generation?

This problem was to puzzle Darwin for the rest of his life, though he speculated that social insects were a 'special case' and natural selection acted on the colony as a whole, rather than on individuals.

Social behaviour has evolved independently at least 11 times in the Hymenoptera (ants, wasps and bees) and only once in other insects, the termites. There must be something special about hymenopterans which predisposes them to sociality.

We now know that even in the social Hymenoptera, natural selection acts on individuals rather than on the colony as a whole. And the answer to Darwin's dilemma lies in a peculiar detail of how sex is determined in ants, wasps and bees.

Females are derived from fertilized eggs, in the usual way. They have the normal number of chromosomes and are said to be diploid. Males, on

Left in a person's finger, the sting of a honeybee worker, Apis mellifera *(UK), continues to pump venom into the wound.*

the other hand, are derived from unfertilized eggs; they have half the normal complement of chromosomes and are said to be haploid. A male hymenopteran is thus in the bizarre position of having a single maternal grandfather but no father, and all his sperms are genetically identical.

This method of sex determination is called haplo-diploidy and it distorts the degree of genetic relatedness between relations: hymenopteran sisters share 75 per cent of their genes by common descent, but only 50 per cent with their daughters. And the pay-off, in genetic terms, for the non-reproductive worker is as follows: although she spends her life contributing to the rearing of sisters, some of which will become queens, and although she may ultimately sacrifice her life in defence of the colony, she nevertheless contributes to her own reproductive success, *even though* she never lays eggs.

This is not a paradox. Because she is more closely related to sisters (75 per cent) than she would be to her own daughters (50 per cent), she is getting a greater proportion of genes identical with her own into the next generation than if she had daughters. It does not matter whether the genes which are passed on are in her body or in the eggs of her sisters: 75 per cent of them are identical. This is the basis of what is called kin selection theory and it is the most elegant explanation for the multiple evolution of sociality in the Hymenoptera. It means that, driven by the tyranny of the genes, the worker is being selfish rather than altruistic. And it solves Darwin's dilemma.

Such a valuable resource is worth protecting, even if it means suicide for the defending workers. But this kamikaze policy is of direct personal benefit to those bees which lose their lives: they are, in fact, being selfish rather than selfless (see box opposite).

After guard duty, the bee spends the rest of her six-week life as a field bee, foraging for pollen and nectar. During this period, she calls upon her considerable powers of information processing to communicate the sources of pollen and nectar to her fellow foragers, using the famous dance language.

These sequences of age-related behaviours undergone by worker honeybees are not inflexible. If the colony is attacked and damaged by a large predator such as a honey badger, the age structure of the colony can be disrupted. In this case, the range of duties is reallocated and bees that were once guards may reactivate their royal jelly glands and revert to being nurses. In this way, the functional integrity of colony life is restored. And the ability of the colony as a whole to respond and adapt to crises is one of the many secrets of the honeybee success story.

When the colony becomes very populous, the effects of queen substance are diluted and the workers prepare to divide the colony by setting in train a series of events which will result in the colony issuing a swarm. They begin to construct queen cells, which are much larger than those for workers. The queen is escorted to these by her entourage and she lays a single egg in each one. There is nothing special about the egg; under different circumstances, it would develop into a worker larva. But the larva which emerges from this egg is fed entirely on queen substance and, 22 days later, a new queen emerges.

The first thing she does is to seek out and sting to death any rival queens which are nearing maturity. Then she leaves the nest to mate.

On her return, the old queen prepares to leave the nest for ever, with a swarm of workers. The swarm, with the queen at its centre, clusters on a branch or rock outcrop while scouts search for a new nest site. On their return, they 'dance the good news' (see pages 58–9) on the surface of the clustering swarm and communicate the whereabouts of the new nest site. The swarm then leaves for their new home.

At the height of her powers, the honeybee queen lays about 1500 eggs per day, She may live as long as five years but, eventually, age takes its toll and she produces less queen substance. The workers react by rearing several new queens and the same swarming process occurs.

WASPISH PAPERWORK

Species of *Polistes,* the paper wasp, are found worldwide, in both temperate and tropical climates. One species, *P. canadensis*, extends from Canada to South America.

All species make paper nests comprising a single comb suspended by a stalk from a branch or underside of a leaf. Ants are the worst enemies of these wasps; to repel them, the wasps smear the suspending stalk with a shiny black secretion from abdominal glands. To make the paper for their nests, the wasps strip fibres off dead wood, chew them and mix them with saliva. They mould this papier mâché into the hexagonal cells which form the main comb of the nest.

Each nest is founded by a mated female. In many species, the female rears a first generation of all-female brood by herself. These become workers and take over the tasks of nest extension and collecting insect food for the larvae. There is no visible difference between these workers and the founding queen, which now rarely leaves the nest and spends most of her time laying eggs. There is, however, one major internal difference between them: the ovaries of the workers do not develop. They are kept in this undeveloped state by a variety of ritualized behaviours on the part of the queen or by her aggression towards them; this takes the form of head butting and shoulder charging. The exact means by which the queen exerts this psychological dominance depends on the species concerned. It is not always 100 per cent successful, and occasionally a worker manages to lay eggs. Because the egg-laying workers are virgins, they lay unfertilized eggs which, like those of all ants, wasps and bees, develop into males.

In some species, the founding queen is joined by other mated females. These auxiliaries lay eggs as well as the queen, but she eats as many of the eggs as she can. Indeed, each individual female can identify eggs laid by rivals and eats them. Ultimately, the one which becomes the dominant queen does so at the apex of a dominance hierarchy which is based on differential egg-eating: she who eats most eggs will be queen.

The workers forage for insect prey and chew it up into a pulpy mass or bolus and they feed the larvae progressively; a forager with food signals willingness to feed larvae by knocking her head against the rim of the cell and buzzing. The larva responds by regurgitating a

ABOVE: *Workers of* P. cavapyta *(Argentina), use their jaws to divide up a ball of chewed caterpillar brought to the nest by a returning forager.*

BELOW: *One of the* P. cavapyta *workers now offers a piece of the food to a larva in its cell. Larvae solicit food by rasping their jaws on the sides of the cell.*

drop of saliva. The worker then holds the food bolus at the entrance to the cell and the larva bites off a piece. The larval saliva is absorbed by the remains of the bolus, some of which the worker will eat. This exchange of saliva (trophallaxis) provides the worker with carbohydrates, proteins and, possibly, enzymes it cannot make itself.

Workers and the queen sometimes give the feeding signal without offering food and then go around the comb, imbibing the saliva droplets offered by larvae.

Returning workers are also solicited for food by nest-mates which are higher up in the dominance hierarchy than they are. This can be an aggressive event, with much pushing, shoving and buzzing. The queen is always fed by the workers and never leaves the nest to forage on her own account.

Species of *Polistes* defend their exposed nests with vigour. If a grazing mammal or a person brushes against the comb, the workers rush about making loud buzzing noises and many will attempt to give the interloper a very painful sting.

The details of social life differ between species of *Polistes*, but, to judge from the large number of species worldwide, the basic life-cycle is a very successful one.

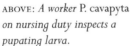

ABOVE: *A worker* P. cavapyta *on nursing duty inspects a pupating larva.*

ABOVE: *A worker* P. cavapyta *fans her wings to create a cooling stream of air over the nest.*

RIGHT: *Dominant workers of* P. cavapyta *force mouth-to-mouth food transfer (trophallaxis) from a subordinate worker just returned to the nest from a foraging trip.*

TERMITES AND ANTS

The colonies of termites and ants can be very much larger than those of honeybees, sometimes numbering in the millions. Much less is understood about their social organization than that of the honeybee.

Unlike the workers of hymenopteran societies, those of termites can be derived from males as well as females. Apart from 'simple' workers, there are often soldier castes, also of both sexes. Caste determination is complex; the allocation of newly emerged nymphs to particular subgroups such as soldiers is in response to immediate colony needs, and is controlled by hormones and pheromones in highly complex and, as yet, incompletely understood ways.

The worst enemies of termites are marauding ants, and termite soldiers are equipped to deal with them in two main ways. Some, such as species of *Coptotermes*, have massively developed heads and powerful jaws. Others, such as those of *Nasutitermes* spp., have virtually lost their jaws. Instead, the front of the head is in the form of a long narrow spout, the nasus, which connects to a large gland. This produces a very sticky liquid which the soldier squirts over any ant, literally stopping it in its tracks.

Unlike the males of social Hymenoptera, those of termites remain with the queen after mating. In some species, the queen becomes a grotesque, pulsating and swollen egg-laying machine, incapable of moving. She depends on workers entirely for food and grooming. And she remains attended by her mate, the king.

Because termites have an incomplete metamorphosis, the larvae or nymphs are miniature versions of adults and are very active, unlike the legless and helpless larvae of hymenopterans. In the lower termites, which depend on gut symbionts to digest the cellulose in their diets, the juveniles obtain and constantly top-up their protozoan helpmates by eating the faeces of adults.

In the higher termites, the digestion of cellulose is carried out by fungi, which the termites cultivate in vast combs. The species of fungi are known only from the nests of termites, so the symbiosis must be millions of years old. Foraging workers return with vegetation, often grasses but sometimes crop plant material, and use this to build up a compost on which the fungus grows.

Termite workers are blind and find their way back from foraging

OPPOSITE: *This 6m (20ft) mound of a termite,* Macrotermes *sp. (Kenya), is made of a mixture of termite droppings and soil.*

AIR CONDITIONING: KEEPING IT COOL

A large, populous colony of termites, ants, wasps or bees can become a very hot place. The activities and metabolism of some thousands to millions of individuals generate heat. In the case of fungus-growing termites and ants (see page 192), the process of humus breakdown by the fungi also generates heat. Add to this the fact that most species live in the tropics and many in deserts and hot, dry savannahs, and it is easy to see that heat can become a problem. Social insects, though, have arrived at a number of ingenious ways to cool down themselves and their nests.

The workers of wasps and bees do this by fanning their wings near the entrance. In this way, they direct a flow of cooling air over the combs. If necessary, they can enhance the cooling process by collecting droplets of water in their crops and then depositing them in strategic places around the nest. By fanning air over these droplets, the water evaporates and the wasps and bees enjoy the benefits of evaporative cooling.

The workers of ants and termites are wingless and so cannot use fanning to cool the nest. They have arrived at two very different solutions to the same problem.

Ants that live in subterranean nests exploit the fact that, even in desert soils, the temperature a few centimetres below the surface remains constant and soil temperature decreases with depth. Ants therefore excavate nests which have a range of depths. The ants simply move downwards as temperatures increase beyond tolerable limits. Conversely, they migrate upwards in the early mornings to benefit from the warmth of the sun.

Termites have the most sophisticated ways of keeping cool, their nests designed to provide air conditioning (see diagram above). Their huge air-conditioning towers are major features in many tropical savannah landscapes. The nests themselves are underground in a complex system of chambers and galleries.

In the extreme deserts of Northern Australia, the magnetic or compass termite, *Amitermes meridionalis*, is so called because it builds wedge-shaped nests, 3.5m (11.5ft) high, arranged along a north–south axis. While the morning and evening sun strikes the nest broadside on, warming it up, during the main heat of the day the sun is directly overhead and only the narrow top of the nest is directly exposed.

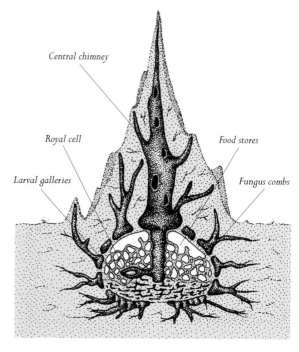

Central chimney

Royal cell

Larval galleries

Food stores

Fungus combs

ABOVE: *A vertical section through the nest mound of the African termite,* Macrotermes bellicosus, *showing the complex fungus garden and the network of chimney spaces through which hot air rises as part of the termites' sophisticated air-conditioning system.*

BELOW: *A computer-generated simulation of the special vanes in the termites' nest, a vital part of the air-conditioning process. Worker termites keep the vanes damp, so the warm air passing over them is cooled down as the water droplets evaporate.*

The mounds of some species are huge – 7.5m (25ft) high in the case of *Macrotermes bellicosus*, in Africa. The earth mound is built above the nest chambers and fungus comb. Hot air from these living quarters rises and flows up a central chimney and from there, via side branches, to a system of thin-walled tunnels in the outer wall. Here, where there are only a few millimetres of outer wall, the air cools, carbon dioxide diffuses outwards and fresh air diffuses inwards. The continuous flow is maintained by pressure from the hotter air rising from the nest proper.

The flow of air now enters a large chamber beneath the surface of the soil, passing between a series of large vanes which the termites keep damp. This dampness cools by evaporation and the fresh air passes back into the living area.

It is remarkable that the worker termites have constructed the equivalent of, in human terms, a skyscraper 9.6km (6 miles) high. And they are blind.

The air-conditioning systems of termites are so effective that human engineers are now constructing buildings with cooling systems based on termite design.

ABOVE: *A mushroom-shaped mud nest of a termite,* Cubitermes *sp., in a Gambian rainforest. The domed top provides protection from torrential rain.*

RIGHT: *A massive turret-like nest mound of a termite,* Macrotermes *sp., in savannah (South Africa). The turret is part of the termites' air-conditioning system.*

A white nymph and four soldiers of the termite Trinervitermes gratiosus *(Kenya). The massive heads of the soldiers are packed with muscles which operate the black, curved jaws. The galleries of the subterranean nest are composed of the termites' own droppings mixed with soil.*

trips by following a scent trail laid down on the outward journey.

Fungus gardens and scent trails are also the forte of ants. Leafcutter ants of Central and South America collect pieces of green leaf which they cut with large, scissor-like jaws. Back at the nest, they add this to a compost for their own species of cultivated fungus, on which they feed.

Although the workers of most ants have eyes, their vision is not acute and they rely on scent trails when foraging. Blind workers and soldiers are found in the massive colonies of the South American army ants, *Eciton burchelli*, and in the African driver ants, *Dorylus nigricans*.

An army ant colony may number 700 000 individuals; only the males and queens have eyes. A colony may send out a swarm raid comprising 150 000 blind ants, in a column 105m (400ft) long and 8m (26ft) wide, all following trails laid down by scout workers. They prey voraciously on any small animals, whether insects or mammals, which they encounter, flushing them out from leaf litter and undergrowth.

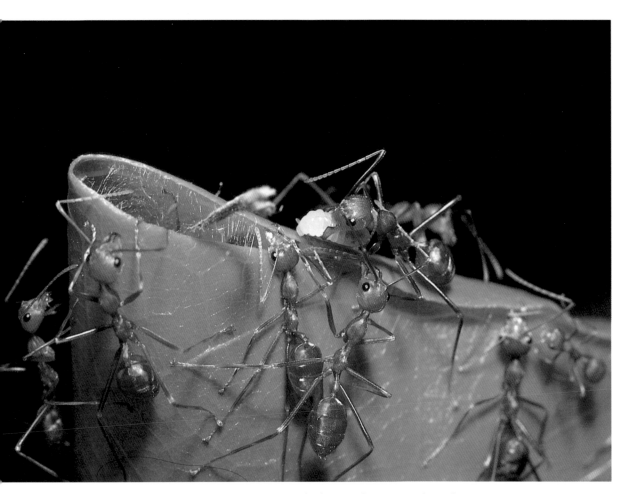

Although a colony of *Eciton burchelli* may lodge in the same place for up to three weeks, mostly it remains on the march, resting in temporary bivouacs.

The African driver ant, *Dorylus nigricans*, occupies the same niche as the army ant of South America. It too has swarm raids which march on a broad front. They are major predators of termites and can even deal with lizards and snakes. *Dorylus* will kill and dismember any large domestic animals such as chickens, goats and pigs if these are tethered or if they are injured and cannot make their escape.

Social insects exert a commanding presence in many of the world's habitats. The workers from a single honeybee colony may visit 2–3 million flowers in a day; the total biomass of termites in the African savannahs greatly exceeds that of the huge herds of zebras, wildebeest and all the other grazing mammals. And ants are the dominant middle-level predators, accounting for more flesh than all the carnivorous mammals.

A worker weaver ant, Oecophylla smaragdina *(Nepal), forms a nest by using a larva as a shuttle to bind two leaves together with silk. The silk is extruded by the larva from glands in the head.*

INSECTS
AND PEOPLE

Friends or foes?

Ladybirds, Epilachna dregei, *feeding
on aphids,* Transvaal, South Africa.

Two thousand years ago, in the markets of central China, it was possible to buy nests of the weaver ant, *Oecophylla smaragdina*. As we saw in Chapter 7 (page 197) these ants use silk extruded by their larvae to stitch two or more living leaves together to form a nest.

The weaver ant nests were a saleable commodity because the ants are voracious predators: citrus growers hung the nests in their fruit trees and the foraging ants kept the trees free of insect pests.

This is the earliest-known example of biological pest control, the use of natural agents to control crop pests in an environmentally friendly way. It shows that for at least two millennia, people in China had a clear understanding of the ecological importance of insects and how this could be put to beneficial use.

As soon as people started cultivating wild plants as crops, they created conditions ideal for insects, those opportunists *par excellence*. As long as crop plants lived in natural conditions, then a wide range of insect predators and parasites kept the populations of herbivorous insects in check.

A dense mass of the aphid, Macrosiphon albifrons, *on a garden lupin (UK). Mass feeding by aphids can cause severe wilting and stress to cultivated plants.*

As people became more sophisticated growers, cultivating dense fields with just a single crop, the stage was set for some insects to assume pest status: a monoculture represents a food bonanza, and pest species would undergo population explosions which their natural enemies initially failed to control. Eventually, the predators and parasites *would* catch up and the pest problem would be temporarily ameliorated. Nevertheless, insects began to compete with people for food, and ever more frequent cycles of runaway population explosions and crashes made farming in some areas of the world a hit or miss business.

Then, along came insecticides, the chemist's answers to every farmer's dream of pest-free crops. Certainly, DDT and the later generations of insecticides had dramatic initial impacts on the numbers of crop pests. Too liberal a use of pesticides made things worse, though, by upsetting the natural balance. Pesticides do not discriminate between the target species and the useful insects which are the farmer's allies: they also reduced the populations of pollinating insects.

LEFT: *A notorious pest of many glasshouse crops, this infesting whitefly,* Trialeurodes vaporarium, *feeds on tomato plants (UK). Growers now control this pest with a parasitic wasp,* Encarsia formosa.

BELOW: *This maize beetle,* Astylus atromaculatus *(South Africa), is one of many crop pests which have managed to follow their host plant around the world.*

Persistent insecticides polluted water supplies via ground water and entered food chains, adversely affecting a wide range of animals including birds of prey and people.

Meanwhile, the insects began to fight back: they responded by evolving strains which are resistant to certain insecticides, in just the same way that many bacteria developed resistance to antibiotics. DDT was subverted in only a few years. An escalating arms race between insects and chemists began, with the cards stacked very much in the insects' favour: their very high fecundity and short generation time made rapid adaptation that much easier. Responding in this way was nothing new for insects: as we saw in Chapters 4 and 6, they have been locked into chemical warfare and arms races with plants for millions of years.

BELOW: *A vine weevil,* Otiorrhynchus sulcatus *(UK), on a house-plant. This weevil is a common pest also in greenhouses.*

In the 40 years after the introduction of insecticides in the 1940s, about 500 insect species have developed resistance to one or more insecticides. Well-known examples include that bane of potato growers, the Colorado beetle, *Leptinotarsa decemlineata*, and the tobacco budworm, *Heliothis virescens*, which is also a pest of cotton.

REDISCOVERING FRIENDS

Rather belatedly, modern agricultural scientists rediscovered what the Chinese of two thousand years ago knew perfectly well: that pest numbers could be kept within acceptable limits by using the services of insect enemies of the pest. The use of biological control to limit the numbers of crop pests is now widespread and successful: more than 5000 species of natural enemies – predatory beetles, parasitic wasps and flies – have been tested, with 300 now being used regularly and with considerable success in 60 countries. In the USA alone, about 700 species of natural pests have been imported to control more than 50 different pests.

OPPOSITE: *Nymphs of cotton-stainer bugs,* Dysdercus *spp. (Kenya), feeding on fallen cotton fruit. These bugs are a pest because a fungus enters the feeding holes they leave and stains the cotton boll.*

Sometimes, it is the pest which has been accidentally imported. The mole cricket, *Scrapteriscus vicinus*, was inadvertently introduced from Brazil into the warmer parts of the United States at the end of the last century. Here, it is a pest of lawns, golf courses and some crops, by feeding at roots and because of its burrowing activities.

RIGHT: *Caterpillars of the large cabbage white butterfly,* Pieris brassicae *(UK), are a major pest of cabbages.*

ABOVE: *Fortunately, help is at hand in the form of parasitic wasps,* Apantales glomeratus, *females of which here lay eggs in the caterpillars. The developing wasp larvae feed on the caterpillars, eventually killing them.*

If biological control is to be mobilized against such an introduced pest, then it is necessary to go back to its original home and find out what natural enemies afflict it. Eventually, American entomologists discovered a wasp, *Larra americana*, which specializes in attacking the mole cricket in Brazil. The female wasp seeks out the cricket, drives it out of its underground burrow and stings it. She then lays a single egg on the paralysed cricket, and leaves it to its fate.

The paralysis caused by the sting is short-lived and the cricket returns to the protection of its burrow. Here, the wasp egg hatches and the larva eats the mole cricket. This wasp was successfully introduced into the USA, where it keeps the numbers of the mole cricket down to acceptable levels.

Some of the most successful uses of biological control have been among glasshouse crops. For example, tomato and cucumber growers routinely release vast numbers of a tiny parasitic wasp, *Encarsia formosa*, to combat the whitefly, *Trialeurodes vaporarium*. Not only does this bug damage the crop by sucking sap, it also excretes a sticky honeydew, on which a sooty mould fungus develops; this spoils the fruit and shortens the lifespan of the leaves.

Female *Encarsia* come to the aid of growers by laying their eggs in the nymphs of the whitefly; the wasp larva eats the nymph and kills it. The culturing of parasites such as *Encarsia* is a growing industry and the economic benefits of biological control are enormous. Between 1946 and 1986, the net savings in California alone exceeded $100 million.

The savings lie not only in the value of undamaged crops. As well as being environmentally friendly, there is a hidden value to biological control. It is simply more successful and cheaper than the blanket use of pesticides. Moreover, the development of new pesticides is slow and expensive: only one chemical in every thousand which is tested is effective, whereas six out of every hundred natural enemies are a success.

REPAIRING BROKEN CHAINS: FINDING THE MISSING LINK

The fact that biological control works is a reflection of the vital roles that insects play in the ecology of our planet. That importance is seen particularly where there has been a manmade break in the network of ecological relationships. Cattle-ranching in Australia is a good example. Cattle do not occur naturally in Australia: they were introduced by settlers in the last century.

Doing the job it was imported to do, an African dung beetle, Onthophagus ferox, *helps dispose of cattle dung in Australia.*

Cattle produce large amounts of dung and, in their native countries, there is a fauna of dung beetles which disposes of it. There is a range of species, some specializing in processing fresh dung, while others cope with drier, older dung; some species eat and breed in the dung at the soil surface, while others bury it in compacted balls as food for their larvae.

Because cattle do not normally occur in Australia, there were no battalions of dung beetles which had co-evolved with cattle to dispose of the dung. The only dung beetles occurring naturally were those adapted to cope with the hard, dry pellets produced by the largest Australian herbivores, the kangaroos. These native dung beetles could not cope with the soft cowpats produced by the vast herds of cattle. This created problems. Because the dung was not being disposed of, it acted as a superb breeding site for the bush fly, *Musca vetustissima*, which is a serious nuisance to both cattle and people.

The scale of the problem is huge: each cow produces enough dung annually to cover about 5.5 hectares (13.5 acres). Collectively, the 22 million cows in today's Australia produce enough dung each year to cover about 120 million hectares (295.5 million acres), sufficient to cover the entire Australian Capital Territory.

INSECTS AS FOOD

The cry 'Waiter, waiter, there's a fly in my soup!' may reduce a restaurant to a stunned silence, but this repugnance towards the consumption of insects is merely a cultural peculiarity. Somewhere, right now, someone is enjoying entomological cuisine.

About 500 insect species form a regular part of the diet of people all over the world; these include crickets, grasshoppers, locusts, termites, the larvae of beetles, wasps and bees, and the caterpillars of moths.

Hornet larvae and pupae (Vespa spp.), those on the right still in the original comb, on sale at a Thai market (Chiang Mai).

Most insects used as food eat either living or dead plant material. Species which are protected chemically with a foul taste are avoided, the human consumers taking good heed of the warning colours sported by such insects.

Insects are nutritious. They provide between 5 and 10 per cent of the animal protein eaten by many people; they are rich in vitamins, minerals and energy.

In central Angola, people fry termites in palm oil; larvae of the palm weevil are slit open, then fried in oil. The large caterpillars of two species of emperor moths are also widely eaten after being degutted and roasted, sun-dried or boiled in water.

In northern Zambia, the larvae of another emperor moth, locally called *mumpa*, are of great economic importance: people travel long distances to gather the caterpillars, which have a protein content of 60–70 per cent. In Northern Transvaal, the Pedi people prefer mopane worms to beef. These, the dried larvae of the mopane emperor moth, *Imbrasia belina*, have a nutty taste and I can recommend them as a pleasant alternative to salted peanuts as an accompaniment to good malt whisky. In Botswana, the mopane worm industry, based on the hand collection of wild populations, is worth about £4.42 million annually.

Collecting 'bamboo worms', the white caterpillars of a moth, for sale as food (Chiang Mai, Thailand).

Native Australians use a wide range of insects for food, the most famous being the witchety grubs. These are the wood-boring larvae of ghost moths. In the drier parts of Australia, people dig up honeypot ants as a source of sweetness. The ants are specialized workers called repletes; other workers feed them large amounts of nectar and their abdomens become greatly distended. The ant colony uses these honeypot workers as storage vessels; they regurgitate honey when solicited by other workers.

Insects, then, are a regular and useful food for people all over the world. In times of famine, they become a vital standby food, especially when protein is in short supply.

Between 1969 and 1982, an elegant solution was devised and put into practice. A range of dung beetles species from Europe and Africa was introduced into Australia. East Africa, with its huge herds of grazing ungulates, was an ideal source of beetles; over time, many parts of Australia enjoyed enhanced rates of dung disposal and a greatly reduced problem from bush flies.

Another manmade break in a chain of natural, sustaining relationships occurred when settlers in New Zealand began large-scale ranching of sheep and cattle in the last century. The early settlers thought they were in for a bonanza: the climate was just right for growing pasture grasses and lush red clover, ideal forage for animals. There was just one thing missing, a vital link in an all-important ecological chain: the native bees of New Zealand, an impoverished fauna of only 26 species, have tongues which are too short to probe clover flowers for nectar and, therefore, cannot be efficient pollinators of this vital crop for sheep and cattle rearing. Honeybees, too, are not efficient pollinators. As a result New Zealand was for many years a net importer of clover seed.

In the 1880s, someone had a bright idea: four species of bumblebee (*Bombus* spp.) were introduced from southern England and, within five years, New Zealand became a net *exporter* of clover seed, as well as a large-scale producer of lamb, beef and dairy products. It is not widely realized that to a large extent Britain's postwar recovery was aided by access to this cheap produce from New Zealand, all dependent on the services of those bumblebee immigrants and their descendants.

Indeed, as much as 30 per cent of all human food is directly or indirectly dependent on pollination by bees. On a world basis, the value of crops pollinated by bees is $1590 million per year. The pollination services of honeybees alone are worth 50 times the honey crop.

Despite our dependence on bees, about 73 per cent of bee-pollinated crops in North America are not provided with managed honeybees for pollination. This means that the majority of crops in Canada and the United States depend on the entirely *fortuitous* pollination services of honeybees and wild bees. This is potentially a very precarious position to be in. The fact that we blithely accept the situation reflects the underlying reality of life on this planet: we can rely on insects to be there, doing the jobs they do so well and on which we depend.

A female of the tawny mining bee, Andrena fulva, *at a gooseberry flower (UK). Soft fruits are often dependent on the largely unmanaged pollination services provided by wild bees such as this one.*

HONEY HUNTING IN NEPAL

In the high Himalayan valleys of Nepal, there lives a giant honeybee. Very little is known about this bee, and until recently it was thought to be a local variety of *Apis dorsata*, one of the widespread honeybees of India and South East Asia. This enigmatic giant is now regarded as a distinct species and is called *Apis laboriosa*. It has been found also in Bhutan, Sikkim and Yunan.

Like the nests of *A. dorsata*, those of *A. laboriosa* consist of exposed wax combs. But there the resemblance ends. Instead of nesting in trees, *A. laboriosa* builds its huge wax combs in clefts and large fissures in near-vertical cliff faces.

This bee is a true high-altitude specialist. It nests most frequently at between 3000 and 3500m (9843–11 483ft), but nests have been found as high as 4100m (13 452ft).

What is remarkable is that colonies of this bee survive the cold climate of this region, where the temperature mostly ranges between −5°C and 10°C (23°F and 50°F) or colder during most months. Workers of *A. laboriosa* have been seen foraging between October and December, when temperatures are below freezing. Dense fur and large body size enable the individual bees to conserve heat in these cold conditions and, back at the nest, the dense clustering of nest bees keeps the comb and developing brood warm.

The local people take great risks to steal honey from these bees. Professional honey gatherers use rope ladders to climb up to the almost inaccessible nests. This risky business often has them hanging out over sheer drops of 400m (over 1300ft). The fact that people are prepared to take such risks reflects the high value placed on the honey produced by *A. laboriosa*.

RIGHT: *Risking death, a Nepalese honey hunter climbs a rope ladder to reach the exposed combs of the giant Himalayan honeybee,* Apis laboriosa.

BELOW: *Exposed wax honeycombs of the giant Himalayan honeybee.*

ABOVE: *Honey hunters melt down the wax after removing honey from the comb.*

INSECT PRODUCTS

Insects are valuable to people for a wide variety of reasons. Honey, wax and silk are not the only useful products we get from insects. The commercial varnish, shellac, is obtained from a scale insect, *Kerria lacca*, and the red food dye, cochineal, is extracted from another scale insect, *Dactylopius coccus,* which is cultured on *Opuntia* cacti.

There is a growing realization that the venom of honeybees can be a rich source of useful drugs. There has long been a tradition among beekeepers that bee venom prevents or delays the onset of arthritis and can ameliorate its effects. This is based on the folk observation that beekeepers, with their unavoidable professional exposure to stings, seem relatively free from arthritis. Indeed, in Britain and North America, there are centres where it is possible to obtain bee venom therapy for arthritis.

A research team at a London hospital has found that one component of bee venom, Peptide 401, is 100 times more effective in reducing arthritic inflammation than hydrocortisone, the steroid drug commonly used in conventional treatments. It also has none of the unpleasant side-effects of steroids.

ABOVE: *As with the dairy cow, the silkworm moth,* Bombyx mori, *is now an entirely domesticated animal, there being no wild populations. Here the caterpillars feed on mulberry leaves in a silk farm in Thailand.*

BRAZIL NUTS NEED ORCHIDS NEED BEES

When we crack open our Brazil nuts each Christmas, we are handling the results of a bizarre network of bee–plant relationships.

The Brazil nut tree, *Bertholetia excelsa*, grows up to 40m (131ft) high in the tropical forests of Amazonian Brazil and Bolivia. As it takes 30–40 years for each tree to reach the flowering and fruiting stage, it has not been feasible, so far, to cultivate plantations: our Christmas nuts are wild, hand-gathered from the forest floor.

Using grafting techniques, trees have been brought to flowering and fruiting in 10–14 years, but the small plantations based on this practice have had poor yields; the plantation setting does not favour pollination.

The flowers of the Brazil nut are self-incompatible: they need to receive pollen from a different tree to be fertilized. They are pollinated by large, fast-flying, long-tongued bees, females of species of *Euglossa*, *Eulaema* and *Eufresia*. These euglossine bees are brilliantly metallic green, blue or gold. They are long-distance pollinators, flying up to 30km (over 18 miles) on a single foraging trip. This makes them ideal pollinators of tropical forest trees, not least because of a special feature of these forests: while there is a high *diversity* of tree species, with up to 275 species per hectare (111 per acre), there is a corresponding low *density* of species. Thus any two individuals of a given species may be separated by 1–3km.

But the Brazil nut story is more complex than this. Male euglossine bees are attracted to orchids. The orchids produce no nectar. And their pollen is unusable by the bees because it is presented in discrete packages, which the bees cannot handle. Instead, the orchids reward the male bees with scent oils. The bees collect the oils and store them in special tissue in their enlarged hindlegs. Female euglossines are not attracted to the orchids.

It is believed that the bees convert the orchid oils into scents which are attractive to the females. It has been suggested that the males of some euglossines use the scent to attract other males in order to set up a mating display, or lek, which attracts females.

RIGHT: *As two worker ants look on, a metallic-green orchid bee,* Euglossa *sp., approaches an orchid to collect scent, which he will store in his massively enlarged hindlegs.*

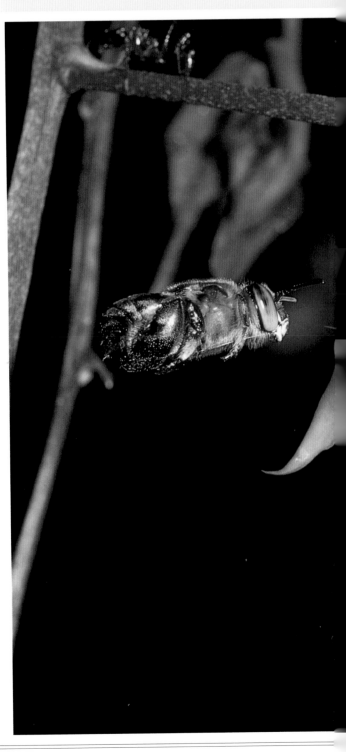

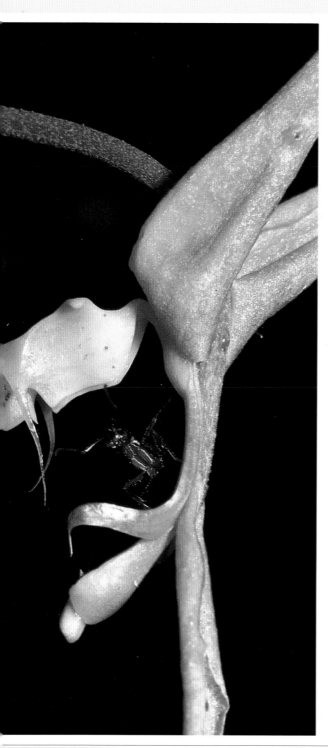

The relationship with orchids is not one-sided. While the male euglossine scrabbles for oil droplets, the orchid deposits a pair of pollen packages or pollinia on his body. When the male visits another flower of the same species, the pollinia adhere to the receptive female part of the flower. Each orchid species has its own unique blend of scents and attracts only a limited, specialist range of males from the local euglossine fauna. In this way, each orchid species reduces the risk of hybridization with other, closely related species.

The Brazil nut industry is of great importance to the economy of Brazil and its neighbours. The nuts are not only exported whole; an oil is extracted from them which is important in the manufacture of cosmetics.

The economic benefits from Brazil nuts are entirely dependent on the services of bees which themselves depend on a diverse flora of orchids for a vital component of their sex lives. Thus, without the orchids, which themselves grow on the branches and trunks of a wide range of tree species, Brazil nuts would not be pollinated. The poor yields of the few Brazil nut plantations may result from a low diversity of bee-sustaining orchids, which is what one might expect in stands of a single tree species of uniform age.

Large-scale agribusiness and forestry in the tropics share a problem with indigenous subsistence farmers: all are in the precarious position of relying on the fortuitous, unmanaged pollinating services of wild bees while having a very incomplete understanding of their conservation and habitat needs.

The pollination of Brazil nut trees raises important questions about forest conservation policies. For example, when a reserve is to be established, is it large enough to support the full range of pollinating insects necessary to sustain it? Is the reserve close enough to other tracts of virgin forest to be within the foraging range of pollinators?

Questions like these need to be answered, for obvious reasons. But, before we can answer them, we need to know so much more about insects and their dynamic relationships with plants and other living things. Meanwhile, the story of Brazil nut pollination is just one potent example of why an understanding of biodiversity and its conservation should be high on our agenda of concern for planet Earth.

UNINVITED GUESTS

Insects have taken advantage of the human propensity to travel and have hitched lifts with us all over the world. One result is that some insect species found themselves in an alien habitat which they were able to exploit much better than their habitat back home. Often, they succeeded because their natural enemies did not join them, or because they found themselves in a very favourable climate. In some cases, insect immigrants were to prove a nuisance; others have turned out to be a boon.

The German wasp, *Vespula germanica*, common all over Europe, including Britain, has enlarged its range dramatically since the late 1950s, due probably to the great increase in air travel. Social wasps have great potential as hitch-hikers: they have an annual life-cycle and the new generation of fertilized queens seeks sheltered spots in which to hibernate when the colony goes into decline in autumn. If these sheltered spots include, say, wooden pallets about to be loaded into the cargo hold of a ship or an aircraft, it is easy to see how queens can be transported around the world. Hibernating queens represent the parent colony's genetic investment in the future. It takes only one queen to survive the winter and found a new nest, and that investment has paid dividends.

In this way, *Vespula germanica* has spread to such remote areas as Ascension Island in the mid Atlantic (mid 1960s) and to New Zealand, where it was first noted in 1944 and now occupies the whole country. It is now known from Tasmania (1959), South Africa (1972), Chile (1974) and Australia (1977). In the United States, it is spreading from its likely point of introduction, the New York area.

In the north of New Zealand, where the wasps do not have to contend with a clearly defined winter, the nests do not go into decline. Instead, they survive the year round and develop to enormous sizes, up to 2.5–3m (8–10ft) across. In such numbers, they are a severe nuisance and pest eradication companies now have special anti-wasp units to deal with the problem.

Auckland, New Zealand: tackling a nest of Vespula germanica, *a major pest.*

Combine human travel with our less appealing habit of dumping car tyres and we have the ideal itinerary for helping the tiger mosquito, *Aëdes* spp., emigrate from South East Asia to the warmer parts of the United States.

This mosquito specializes in breeding in small temporary pools. The small amount of water collected in a halved coconut shell is all it needs. Such small bodies of water are usually very short-lived, but last long enough for the mosquito to complete its life-cycle. Heaps of tyres in dumps also trap water and provide much larger and longer-lasting bodies of water in which the mosquitoes can breed.

Tyre dumps are often situated on the outskirts of cities. So are airports. Mated females of *Aëdes* no doubt caught a flight with connections to the southern USA, where tyre dumps with small pools of water were waiting. In SE Asia, this mosquito transmits certain diseases but, fortunately, it seems that infected adults did not make it to the United States. Nevertheless, it breeds in vast numbers and, as a bloodsucker, is a severe nuisance.

Fortunately, there is another mosquito in SE Asia, *Toxorhynchites* spp., whose larvae develop in the same temporary pools as the *Aëdes*. These larvae are carnivores and eat the *Aëdes* larvae. They are now being introduced into the USA as biological control agents.

Another emigrant from the Old World to the New World has had entirely beneficial effects. This is the alfalfa leafcutter bee, *Megachile rotundata*, which originated in the steppes of eastern Europe and central and south-west Asia. This species nests in old beetle borings in dead wood or hollow plant stems.

No one knows how this little bee made it to the USA, but no doubt pieces of timber with occupied nests found their way by human agency. This was most fortuitous for farmers. Alfalfa (lucerne) is the fourth most valuable crop in North America and is used as forage for cattle. Honeybees are very poor pollinators, but *Megachile rotundata* is a specialist on it and is now reared commercially for alfalfa pollination.

INSECTS AND THE
RECONSTRUCTION OF PAST EVENTS

People have discovered further, less obvious, uses for insects. Archaeologists have developed an interest in entomology because insect cuticle is resistant, persisting for centuries, and insect remains are sometimes common at archaeological sites – they can be just as useful as human artefacts. It is possible to identify the species involved and thus draw up an insect profile of the site. Because insects often have highly specific relationships with particular plant species, including crops, it is possible to use the insect remains to deduce information about the local floras, climate and agricultural practices of long ago.

Insect remains are common also in Pleistocene-age peat bogs and, again, they can give valuable clues as to local climate and plant cover.

Forensic scientists increasingly use insects in their attempts to solve crime. For example, insect remains mixed up with illegally imported cannabis give valuable clues to the origin of the drug and sometimes enable the route of importation to be deduced.

Insects which feed on and breed in corpses can yield much useful information, which may be especially helpful in solving murder investigations. When a dead body decays, it undergoes a distinct succession of stages, the timing and duration of which depend on temperature, humidity and light levels. Each stage is characterized by a particular assemblage of insect species, a mixture of flies and beetles.

When a human corpse is discovered under suspicious circumstances, the insect fauna present can be very informative. The age and size of the fly larvae enable the time of death to be estimated. The actual species present may give other vital clues. For example, some corpse flies will lay eggs only in direct sunlight, others only in shade. Thus, the mix of species may indicate if the corpse has been moved after death and therefore may be the first hint that a murder has in fact been committed.

Whether we use insects as biological control agents, import useful species across the world, or make use of their own products, we lift them out of one context and place them in another, co-opting their specialist roles to support or enhance our own ecology. The fact that insects are such precise specialists enables archaeologists and forensic scientists to use insect remains to glean useful information.

INSECTS: SOME VITAL STATISTICS
FOR PLANET EARTH

The insects' tendency to be ultra-specialists should alert us to the fact that we need to understand more of the complex relationships between insects and the rest of the living world, not least because we are even more dependent on the unmanaged ecological services of entire insect faunas: they play central roles in the dynamics of entire ecosystems.

Without insects, we would be inundated with dead plant and animal material. Of course, insects are not alone in this: they work in tandem with bacteria and fungi. Nevertheless, they are vital links in the processes which return nutrients to the soil and, especially, as plant eaters: insects are the world's most important herbivores. Fifty per cent of all green plant material is ultimately consumed by insects and processed into nutrients. In North American forests ants are responsible for turning over more soil than earthworms.

Insects are the major middle-level predators in almost all terrestrial habitats. They process more flesh than all the large carnivores – crocodiles and alligators, lions, tigers and wolves – put together.

The ecological impact of insects is mind-numbing in its extent: the daily weight of food eaten by a large swarm of the African desert locust, *Schistocerca gregaria*, is nearly four times that eaten by the human population of New York or Greater London. The honeybees introduced by people from the Old World into the tropics of South America are responsible for moving 21 billion kg (46 billion lb) of pollen and 23 billion kg (50 billion lb) of nectar each year; in so doing, they augment the pollinating activities of the native bee fauna. And this has aesthetic implications, too: much of the visual impact of our planet is the direct result of the interaction between flowering plants and the insects that pollinate them.

From the human viewpoint, there is a negative side to the impact made by insects: as the major plant eaters, they compete directly with us for food. The locust swarm can still leave famine in its wake. And millions of people die each year from insect-borne diseases such as malaria – in fact, one in six humans is suffering from an insect-borne disease.

Nevertheless, we need to conserve insects. In saying this, we really mean that we need to conserve habitats. Although the aesthetic arguments for doing so would be sufficient to justify environmental

OPPOSITE: *A warningly coloured grasshopper,* Poekilocerus vittatus *(Saudi Arabia), roosts on an iris flower.*

concerns, we should also be motivated by enlightened self-interest: in recognizing that we are ultimately dependent on insects, we acknowledge our reliance on maintaining biodiversity. Many more useful insects and insect products remain to be discovered, especially in those biodiversity hotspots, the tropical rainforests. Indeed, four-fifths of all known plant species and half of all known animal species live in the forests of the humid tropics.

Unfortunately, we do not act on this knowledge. Less than half of the original 16 million square kilometres (6.18 million square miles) of tropical rainforest survives. At the present rate of attrition, the forests of Amazonia will be lost in 40 years. Nigerian forests are now logged out. Of the 56 countries which traditionally exported luxury timbers to the over-developed world, 23 are now net importers of timber. We are ransacking the planet faster than we increase our understanding of how it works. And the loss of each tract of forest means the loss of yet another opportunity to learn more of those life-sustaining relationships between insects and other living things.

We can regard the dense network of relationships between living organisms as a very complex piece of architecture. Within this structure, insects occupy keystone positions: remove them, and the whole edifice collapses. This brings us back to our original point about dinosaurs and people existing by courtesy of the insects. It is literally true. Our ancestors in Africa were able to exploit the opportunities presented by habitats which were largely created and sustained by the interactions between insects and plants. All that we hold to be human was possible because of this fundamental fact of life on earth.

Insects, then, exert a commanding presence in a way that smells very strongly of success. And the conservation of insects and their habitats should be of the highest priority if we are to continue to share in the benefits of that success.

It is a chilling thought that insects and the rest of this planet can survive perfectly well without us, but we cannot survive without them.

GLOSSARY

Technical terms have been kept to a minimum and many are explained in the text. The following occur more frequently, sometimes without definition.

Chitin A complex polysaccharide, forming a horny substance, which is the major component of the cuticle of insects; it forms the bulk of the outer shell or exoskeleton of insects and their relatives.

Cuticle The external, secreted, multi-layered shell of an insect, comprising a mixture of chitin and protein.

Endoskeleton Literally, an inner skeleton, the internal supporting framework of fish, birds and mammals.

Exoskeleton Literally, an outer skeleton, the external, secreted shell or supporting framework of crustacea, scorpions, spiders and insects.

Pheromone A volatile chemical released by an animal which affects the behaviour of another animal, e.g. mate-attracting sex pheromones, and alarm pheromones which recruit additional ant, wasp or bee workers to the defence of their colony.

Sensillum (pl. **sensilla**) A sense organ, which might be a single, isolated structure, such as a sensory bristle, or part of a more complex structure, such as a compound eye.

Spiracle A breathing pore, an external opening of the system of breathing tubes or tracheae.

Sternum (pl. **sterna**) The lower (ventral) surface of a body segment.

Tarsus (pl. **tarsae**; adj. **tarsal**) The leg section furthest from the body, consisting of one to five segments, the last of which bears a pair of claws.

Tergum (pl. **terga**) The upper (dorsal) surface of a body segment.

Thorax The middle of the three body divisions of an insect, bearing the wings and six legs.

Trachea (pl. **tracheae**) One of the system of tubes which conducts oxygen from the spiracles (breathing pores) to all tissues, and carbon dioxide from tissues to the exterior.

Tracheole An ultra-fine tracheal tube.

FURTHER READING

G. C. McGavin, *Insects of the Northern Hemisphere,* Dragon's World, Limpsfield & London (1992).

G. C. McGavin, *The Pocket Guide to Insects of the Northern Hemisphere*, Dragon's World, Limpsfield & London (1992).

G. C. McGavin, *Bugs of the World*, Blandford Press–Cassell, London (1993).

C. O'Toole, *Insects in Camera: A Photographic Essay on Behaviour*, Oxford University Press, Oxford (1985).

C. O'Toole (ed.), *The Encyclopaedia of Insects*, Unwin Animal Library Vol. 6, Allen & Unwin, London (1986).

C. O'Toole and A. Raw, *Bees of the World*, Blandford Press–Cassell, London (1991).

K. Preston-Mafham, *Grasshoppers and Mantids of the World*, Blandford Press–Cassell, London (1990).

R. Preston-Mafham and K. Preston-Mafham, *Butterflies of the World*, Blandford Press, London (1988).

A. Wootton, *Insects of the World*, Blandford Press, Poole (1984).

PICTURE CREDITS

INDEX